How to Use This Book

KEY TO SYMBOLS

➕ Map reference to the accompanying fold-out map

✉ Address

☎ Telephone number

🕐 Opening/closing times

🍴 Restaurant or café

🚉 Nearest rail station

Ⓜ Nearest subway (Metro) station

🚌 Nearest bus route/streetcar

⛴ Nearest riverboat or ferry stop

♿ Facilities for visitors with disabilities

❓ Other practical information

▷ Further information

ℹ Tourist information

✋ Admission charges: Expensive (more than $20), Moderate ($11–$20), and Inexpensive ($10 or less)

This guide is divided into four sections
• Essential Toronto: An introduction to the city and tips on making the most of your stay.
• Toronto by Area: We've broken the city into five areas, and recommended the best sights, shops, entertainment venues, nightlife and restaurants in each one. Suggested walks help you to explore on foot.
• Where to Stay: The best hotels, whether you're looking for luxury, budget or something in between.
• Need to Know: The info you need to make your trip run smoothly, including getting about by public transport, weather tips, emergency phone numbers and useful websites.

Navigation In the Toronto by Area chapter, we've given each area its own color, which is also used on the locator maps throughout the book and the map on the inside front cover.

Maps The fold-out map accompanying this book is a comprehensive street plan of Toronto. The grid on this fold-out map is the same as the grid on the locator maps within the book. We've given grid references within the book for each sight and listing.

Contents

Introducing Toronto

When most people think of Canada, they think of its vast, natural beauty, and forget about its multicultural metropolises. Among the top entertainment capitals, Toronto is vibrant, vivacious, good looking… a definite A-list destination.

The A-list come here, too, from all over the world, especially for the film festival. Ottawa may be the nation's capital, but Toronto is where it's at, and neither the soaring cost of real estate nor the summer smog that occasionally covers downtown has stopped it becoming North America's fourth-largest city and Canada's premier tourist destination.

Immigrants still arrive at the rate of around 100,000 a year, and their diversity has made Toronto one of the most multicultural cities in the world. This is no melting pot, though; it's a honeycomb of colorful neighborhoods offering a world of atmospheres, from exotic Asian enclaves to leafy streets with all the laid-back ambience of old Europe. The tensions that mar many immigrant-heavy cities are conspicuously absent and though there are a few no-go areas after dark, Toronto is generally safe and friendly. The city's motto says it all: Diversity our Strength.

An air of enthusiasm pervades the city. Downtown is populated by a mix of dynamic business people and laid-back individals, but they all share a common desire for their city to be best (and preferably first) at everything. This extends to their "green" credentials, the size and quality of their museums and galleries, the plethora of home-grown talent in the arts and entertainment world, and the achievements of their scientists and academics.

Toronto has many attractions, but to get a real feel for the city it's just as important simply to hang out on a restaurant patio, on the lakeshore, or at one of the hundreds of festivals or free concerts.

Facts + Figures

- Toronto is on the same latitude as the French Riviera.
- Nearly half of Toronto's 2.9 million population were born outside of Canada.
- Toronto has more than 600km (373 miles) of cycling trails.

INSIDER INFORMATION

There's nothing like visiting a city with someone who knows their way around it, as they usually know all the best places to go, but if you don't have a friend in Toronto, don't despair. The TAP into TO! scheme provides (for free) a knowledgeable local to guide you around and share some of their own city secrets. Call 416/338-2786 for information.

A RECORD LOST

For more than 30 years Toronto's CN Tower ruled supreme as the tallest free-standing building in the world, but in 2010 it was knocked into third place by the Burj Khalifa in Dubai (at 829.8m/2,722ft) and the Canon Tower in China (at 600m/1,969ft). The CN Tower stands at 553.3m (1,815.5ft).

HOLLYWOOD NORTH

A huge number of movies and TV shows are filmed in Toronto each year. With a wealth of exciting backdrops, popular locations include the Distillery Historic District (*Chicago, Cinderella Man, Suits*) and Casa Loma, which was the interior of the X-Men's "school for gifted youngsters." Dundas Street featured in *Hairspray* and *The Incredible Hulk* (Edward Norton, Liv Tyler) and *Repo Men* (Jude Law).

A Short Stay in Toronto

DAY 1

Morning You might as well start out with a visit to the **CN Tower** (▷ 26–27) or it will constantly beckon from wherever else you are in the city. Arrive in good time for the 9am opening, and go all the way to the top for a spectacular view of Toronto.

Mid-morning Walk west along Front Street to Spadina, then take a streetcar north to Dundas to visit the spectacular **Art Gallery of Ontario** (AGO, ▷ 24–25), a showcase of both art and architecture.

Lunch Lunch at the AGO for a fine dining experience within the Frank Gehry extension on Dundas Street. Canadian art adorns the walls and local Canadian produce is on the menu. For a lighter meal, the café downstairs is equally good.

Afternoon Take the streetcar back down Spadina all the way to the lake-shore, then stroll east to take the ferry to **Toronto Islands** (▷ 64–65). Rent a bicycle or just stroll through the parkland, relax on one of the sandy beaches and perhaps take a dip in the lake.

Dinner Dress up and head to the **Canoe Restaurant and Bar** (▷ 57; 54th Floor TD Bank Tower, 66 Wellington Street West; tel: 416/364-0054). This is one of Canada's finest restaurants, with excellent food and superb views, so make sure you have a reservation.

Evening Take in a Broadway-style show, concert or comedy night, then join the after-theater crowd at any place in the Entertainment District that appeals. The choice there includes chic cocktail lounges, pubs, jazz clubs and dance clubs, and you can just stroll until you see (or hear) something you like.

DAY 2

Morning Pick up a typical Toronto breakfast of a peameal bacon sandwich at **St. Lawrence Market** (▷ 51) then walk west along Front Street to Union Station and take the subway up to the Museum stop to visit the **Royal Ontario Museum** (ROM, ▷ 82–83).

Mid-morning After the museum, walk north across Bloor Street to explore the many upscale stores on the leafy streets of **Yorkville** (▷ 86).

Lunch Le Paradis Restaurant (166 Bedford Road, tel: 416/921-0995; lunch served Tue–Fri only) is a chic brasserie/bistro with a good-value fixed-price lunch.

Afternoon Take the subway to Dupont, then walk up to visit **Casa Loma** (▷ 78–79). Later, make your way to Greektown and stroll along Danforth Avenue to soak up the European atmosphere of one of Toronto's most vibrant neighborhoods.

Dinner Dine in style at the renowned **Pan restaurant** (516 Danforth Avenue, tel: 416/466-8158), where traditional Greek dishes are on the menu and the superb wine list includes a worldwide selection, including Greek.

Evening Head back downtown for late-night live music at **Massey Hall** (▷ 56), a National Historic Site yet still full of rock 'n' roll and with a great ambience. Alternatively, another great night out is to see the 10.30 show at **Second City** comedy club (▷ 38), Friday or Saturday only, both in the Entertainment District.

Top 25

►►►

Art Gallery of Ontario
▷ 24–25 One of Canada's principal art galleries, strong in Canadian art.

Bata Shoe Museum
▷ 76–77 Fascinating collection of shoes through the ages.

Black Creek Pioneer Village ▷ 96 A complete small rural community replicating Victorian Ontario.

Yorkville ▷ 86 Toronto's chicest neighborhood and a true shopper's delight.

University of Toronto ▷ 84–85 A venerable institution with an impressive roster of alumni.

Toronto Zoo ▷ 102 Animals from every continent roam spacious enclosures that try to re-create their natural habitats.

Toronto Islands ▷ 64–65 These peaceful islands with sandy beaches are just a short ferry ride away from downtown.

St. Lawrence Market ▷ 51 This historic market building offers a wonderful assortment of food.

Ripley's Aquarium of Canada ▷ 31 Get up close to sharks, rays and more.

Royal Ontario Museum ▷ 82–83 Canada's largest museum contains 6 million objects, including a superb collection of Chinese art.

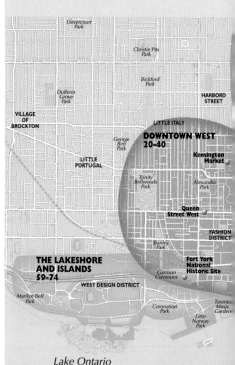

Queen Street West ▷ 32 Vibrant area with trendy clothing stores galore, plus lively patios, bars and cafes.

Ontario Science Centre ▷ 100–101 Nine superb exhibition halls packed with interactive displays.

These pages are a quick guide to the Top 25, which are described in more detail later. Here they are listed alphabetically, and the tinted background shows which area they are in.

Canada's Wonderland ▷ 98–99 Canada's premier theme park, with 200 attractions.

Casa Loma ▷ 78–79 An 18th-century fairy-tale castle built for an early-20th-century millionaire.

City Hall ▷ 44–45 Instantly recognizable, the futuristic-looking City Hall was designed in the 1960s.

The CN Tower ▷ 26–27 An iconic building with one of the world's highest viewing platforms.

Design Exchange ▷ 46–47 Graceful Moderne building now dedicated to Canadian design.

Distillery Historic District ▷ 48–49 Former distillery buildings now given over to culture.

Fort York ▷ 28–29 Historic spot where the city was founded in 1793.

Gardiner Museum ▷ 80 Superb museum with lots to see devoted to ceramic art, from pre-Columbian to the present.

Harbourfront Centre ▷ 62–63 Docklands, now revitalized as a commercial, cultural and leisure center.

Hockey Hall of Fame ▷ 50 A shrine to Canada's sporting obsession.

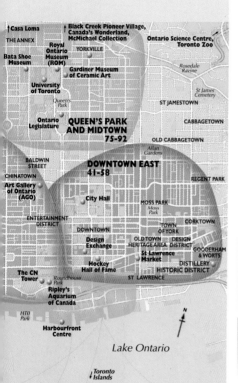

Map labels:
- Casa Loma
- THE ANNEX
- Bata Shoe Museum
- University of Toronto
- Black Creek Pioneer Village, Canada's Wonderland, McMichael Collection
- Royal Ontario Museum (ROM)
- YORKVILLE
- Gardiner Museum of Ceramic Art
- Queen's Park
- Ontario Legislature
- Ontario Science Centre, Toronto Zoo
- Rosedale Ravine
- St James Cemetery
- ST JAMESTOWN
- **QUEEN'S PARK AND MIDTOWN 75–92**
- CABBAGETOWN
- OLD CABBAGETOWN
- BALDWIN STREET
- Allan Gardens
- **DOWNTOWN EAST 41–58**
- CHINATOWN
- REGENT PARK
- Art Gallery of Ontario (AGO)
- City Hall
- MOSS PARK
- Moss Park
- ENTERTAINMENT DISTRICT
- DOWNTOWN
- TOWN OF YORK
- CORKTOWN
- Design Exchange
- OLD TOWN HERITAGE AREA
- DESIGN DISTRICT
- St Lawrence Market
- GOODERHAM & WORTS
- Hockey Hall of Fame
- DISTILLERY
- The CN Tower
- Roundhouse Park
- ST LAWRENCE
- HISTORIC DISTRICT
- Ripley's Aquarium of Canada
- HTO Park
- Harbourfront Centre
- Lake Ontario
- N
- Toronto Islands

Ontario Legislature ▷ 81 The home of the government of the province of Ontario.

McMichael Canadian Art Collection ▷ 97 Influential works of the Group of Seven artists.

Kensington Market ▷ 30 The perfect place to experience Toronto's vibrant multiculturalism.

ESSENTIAL TORONTO TOP 25

▲▲▲

◀ ◀ ◀

Shopping

If you love to shop, come to Toronto with a fat wallet and a spare suitcase. The possibilities are seemingly endless, and you could shop every day for a month and still not discover all the quirky backstreet boutiques, cutting-edge products and highly individual craftworks.

From Malls to Markets

Among the particular pleasures of shopping here are the ease of getting around and the friendly staff. Add to this the delightful neighborhoods with specialty stores, the number of glittering malls and the traditional markets and you've got something really special. Even in the Financial District, the skyscraper towers often harbor one or more floors of shopping at street level.

Fashion

Most of the world's top names in fashion have found a home in Toronto, particularly on the "mink mile" (Bloor Street between Avenue Road and Yonge Street). Chanel, Max Mara, Hermès, Gucci, Prada, Louis Vuitton, to name a few, have seasonal windows. Diamonds, watches and crystal sparkle at Tiffany's, Royale de Versailles, Cartier and Swarovski. Roots Canada, a giant in casual clothing and sportswear, occupies a large space, and Zara, Spain's popular and stylish budget-conscious entry in the fashion field, is here as well. Still at the heart of Bloor Street is Holt Renfrew, a three-story style emporium for men, women and the home.

A GOOD SMOKE

Canada has never severed diplomatic or trade relations with Cuba, and so just about every tobacconist in Toronto has a humidor full of Havanas—something you won't find anywhere south of the border. But if you'll be crossing into the US anytime soon, smoke those stogies in Canada: US laws embargo trade with Cuba, and trying to take goods across the border could lead to charges.

St. Lawrence Market; shopping in Toronto's stores; Kensington market; colorful downtown fountains (top to bottom)

Arts and Crafts

Bloor Street is not the only game in town. On Spadina Avenue around Dundas, fur and garment manufacturers have showrooms and retail outlets. There are Pan-Asian Shopping Malls in Markham and Scarborough that would not feel out of place in Asia. Toronto's arts and crafts communities show their works on Queen Street West, which abounds with custom jewelers, sophisticated glass sculpture galleries and native and Inuit art. For classy antiques visit Davenport Road at Avenue.

Music

Toronto is proud of its musicians and entertainers, and the huge HMV store on Yonge Street stages live in-store performances. Most Toronto music stores dedicate shelves to Canadian-bred talent such as Bryan Adams, Avril Lavigne, Alanis Morrissette and Shania Twain.

Historic Stores

At Queen's Quay Terminal the Tilley Endurables Shop features the Tilley Hat. Advertised as having been retrieved intact after it was eaten by an elephant, it comes with a lifetime guarantee and owner's manual. Hudson's Bay Company, a former fur trading post that's as old as Canada itself, and now known simply as Hudson's Bay, is a major store selling everything from fur items to appliances, electronics and fashion. You will find a superb range of stores on Bloor and Yonge, as well as in suburban shopping malls.

PICK UP A BARGAIN

There is nothing so satisfying as finding a real bargain, and the best time for this in Toronto is the first day of business after Christmas, when prices are routinely slashed by half (or more). There are sales in summer, too, roughly June through August. Year-round bargains can be found in the discount malls, such as Dixie Outlet Mall. Honest Ed's (581 Bloor West) is a Toronto institution of tackiness but scheduled to close down in 2016.

Shopping by Theme

Toronto is the best city in Canada for shopping and in this book we have selected the best. For a more detailed write-up, see the individual listings in Toronto by Area.

ANTIQUES

Abraham's (▷ 35)
Reflections Vintage & Antiques (▷ 89)
Toronto Antiques on King (▷ 36)

ARTS AND CRAFTS

Bay of Spirits Gallery (▷ 55)
The Centre Shop (▷ 69)
Craft Ontario (▷ 89)
Erin Stump Projects (▷ 35)
Lake View Market (▷ 69)
The Power Plant (▷ 36)
William Ashley China (▷ 89)

BOOKS AND TOYS

The Beguiling Books & Art (▷ panel, 36)
Ben McNally Books (▷ panel, 36, 55)
Book City (▷ panel, 36)
Rolo (▷ 89)
The Monkey's Paw (▷ 36)

CLOTHES FOR MEN

Bulloch Tailors (▷ 55)
From Hockey to Hollywood (▷ 35)
GOTStyle (▷ 35)
Harry Rosen (▷ 89)
Haven (▷ 55)
M0851 (▷ 89)
Stollery's (▷ 89)
Tilley Endurables (▷ 69)

CLOTHES FOR WOMEN

Cabaret (▷ 35)
Club Monaco (▷ 35)
Freda's (▷ 35)
Fresh Collective (▷ 35)
Holt Renfrew (▷ 89)
John Fluevog (▷ 36)
Lavish and Squalor (▷ 36)
M0851 (▷ 89)
Stollery's (▷ 89)
Tilley Endurables (▷ 69)

FOOD AND DRINK

All the Best Fine Foods (▷ 89)
Daniel et Daniel (▷ 55)
Dish Cooking Studio (▷ 89)
Kitchen Table (▷ 69)
LCBO (▷ 69)
Ten Ren Tea (▷ 36)

HOMEWARES

Bookhou (▷ 35)
Drake General Store (▷ 35)

JEWELRY

Anne Sportun Fine Jewellery (▷ 35)
Corktown Designs (▷ 55)
Silverbridge (▷ 89)

MALLS/DEPARTMENT STORES

Atrium (▷ 55)
Brookfield Place (▷ 55)
College Park (▷ 55)

First Canadian Place (▷ 55)
Holtrenfrew (▷ 89)
Hudson's Bay (▷ 55)
Queen's Quay Terminal (▷ 69)
Toronto Eaton Centre (▷ 55)

MUSIC

Grigorian (▷ 89)
Sonic Boom (▷ 36)

SPORTS

From Hockey to Hollywood (▷ 35)
Mountain Equipment Co-op (MEC) (▷ 36)
Wheel Excitement (▷ 69)

Toronto by Night

Toronto is as lively by night as it is in daylight, only just behind New York and London in the nightlife stakes. There's a theater district (▷ below) and plenty of other theaters around the city. There are several world-class concert halls, stadium rock concerts at the Rogers Centre or Molson Canadian Amphitheatre, atmospheric live venues that leave no musical stone unturned, and a huge choice of nightclubs and bars. The streets are generally safe and public transportation after dark is good.

Clubs, Clubs and More Clubs

The club-lined streets of downtown Toronto are filled until dawn. Many of the city's dance clubs are on the Richmond Street strip just south of Queen West, which is in itself home to a number of the live-music venues. The College Street area is also a good bet for searching out up-and-coming dance bars, though the area, with its many cafés and bistros, is more oriented toward a laid-back lounge crowd. When the clubs close (by 3am) the fearless night owls seek out all-night raves that are publicized only by word of mouth.

Polson Pier

An alternative to the downtown scene is the Polson Pier entertainment complex (▷ 70), out on a limb in the Port of Toronto. It includes Toronto's largest lakeside patio, a concert-equipped nightclub, outdoor amusements and activities, and even a drive-in movie theater.

City Hall; patrons enjoying a drink in a downtown bar; Chinatown (top to bottom)

THEATRE DISTRICT

Since the mid-19th century, the area now known as the Theatre District has been animated with music halls, theaters and entertainment palaces. The opening of the Royal Alexandra Theatre in 1907 breathed life into the area. In 1989 the new SkyDome (now Rogers Centre) brought crowds of up to 55,000 into the district for baseball and other events. Restaurants and entertainment spots began springing up, and the pace hasn't stopped.

Eating Out

Toronto is reputed to have no fewer than 7,000 restaurants, and though these include fast-food joints and neighborhood diners, you are still spoiled for choice with really excellent places to eat. This cosmopolitan city encompasses just about every major culture in its cuisine and prides itself on being Canada's trendsetter.

Neighborhood dining

The famous neighborhoods of Toronto make it easy to find a particular cuisine: Little Italy and Corso Italia; Greektown on the Danforth; Little India; Koreatown; Portugal Village; Little Poland; and a choice of Chinatowns. Shopping neighborhoods, such as Bloor/Yorkville, Yonge Street and the Fashion District, have plenty of eateries, and the Entertainment District is full of places offering pre- and post-show dinners. You can even join the power breakfast set in a Financial District eatery. If you happen upon a place where the locals go, you are guaranteed the best food and a great atmosphere.

Food Festivals

The best times to sample the various cuisines in Toronto is during one of the ethnic festivals: Chinese New Year (Jan/Feb); Taste of Little Italy (Jun); Scotiabank Carribean Carnival Toronto, Taste of the Danforth, Festival of South Asia and MuslimFest (Jul/Aug); and the Bloor West Village Toronto Ukrainian Festival and the Hispanic Fiesta (late Aug/early Sep). Canadian food is on offer at the Canadian National Exhibition (late Aug/early Sep) and the Royal Agricultural Winter Fair (Nov).

TAKE TO THE LAKE

Try a brunch, lunch or dinner cruise. Prices are $45–$90, and some include dancing. Try Mariposa Cruises (tel: 416/203-0178, www.mariposacruises.com); Empress of Canada (tel: 416/260-5665, www.empressofcanada.com); Jubilee Queen (tel: 416/203-7245, www.jubileequeen-cruises.ca); or Great Lakes Schooner (tel: 416/260-6355, www.greatlakesschooner.com).

Chinatown by day; freshly baked bread; Little Italy; alfresco dining in Little Italy (top to bottom)

Restaurants by Cuisine

With more than 7,000 restaurants and cafés, Toronto encompasses cuisines that are as multicultural as the city itself. For a more detailed description of each restaurant, see Toronto by Area.

AFRICAN

The Sultan's Tent & Café Moroc (▷ 58)

CANADIAN/US

360 at the CN Tower (▷ 39, panel, 40)
Canoe (▷ panel, 40, 57)
City Kitchen (▷ panel, 58)
The Harbord Room (▷ 40)
Museum Tavern (▷ 92)
Senator (▷ 58)
Southern Accent (▷ 92)
Tundra (▷ 58)

CHINESE

Dumpling House Restaurant (▷ 39)
Wah Sing (▷ 40)

CONTINENTAL

Alexandros Take-Out (▷ 72)
Future Bistro (▷ 92)
Rectory Café (▷ 72)
Richtree Natural Market (▷ 58)
Scaramouche (▷ panel, 40)

DINER FARE

The Carousel Café (▷ 72)
Fran's (▷ 57)
Urban Eatery (▷ panel, 58)

ECLECTIC/FUSION

Fred's Not Here (▷ 40)
Matahari Bar & Grill (▷ 40)
Senses (▷ 40)

FRENCH

Bb33 (▷ 57)
Bloor Street Diner (▷ 92)
Bymark (▷ 57)
Crème Brasserie (▷ 92)
Frank's Kitchen (▷ 39)
Le Sélect Bistro (▷ 40)
Osgoode Hall Restaurant (▷ 57–58)

ITALIAN

Bar Italia (▷ 39)
Café Diplomatico (▷ 39)
Fieramosca (▷ 92)
Fusaro's Kitchen (▷ 40)

JAPANESE

Ema-Tei (▷ 39–40)
Kokoro Sushi (▷ 72)
Nami (▷ 57)
Wow Sushi (▷ 92)

MEXICAN

Como en Casa (▷ 92)

OTHER EUROPEAN

Chiado (▷ 39)
Esplanade Bier Markt (▷ 57)

PUB AND BAR FOOD

Crush (▷ 39)
Irish Embassy Pub & Grill (▷ 57)
Roof Lounge (▷ panel, 40)

SEAFOOD

Joso's (▷ 92)
Starfish (▷ 58)

STEAKS/GRILLS

Baton Rouge (▷ panel, 58)
Pearl Harbourfront Restaurant (▷ 72)
Harbour Sixty Steakhouse (▷ 72)
Morton's (▷ 92)
Ruth's Chris Steak House (▷ 58)

Top Tips For...

Sometimes, when a city has so much to offer, it's not so easy to focus on your particular interests and find out the best places to go. The following suggestions should help you tailor your ideal visit. Each sight or listing has a fuller write-up in Toronto by Area.

A MEAL WITH A VIEW

Splash out on a meal at 360 (▷ 39) and soak up the views of the entire city as you revolve a full circle high up on the CN Tower.

Pick out a prime spot on a patio at the Pearl Harbourfront Restaurant (▷ 72) at Queen's Quay Terminal (▷ 69) and watch all the activity on the lake.

Get room service at the Renaissance Toronto Downtown hotel (▷ 111) and watch a ball game from a room overlooking the Rogers Centre stadium (▷ 33).

Reserve a window seat at Canoe (▷ 57) and look down over the Financial District while savoring upscale Canadian cuisine.

Canoe restaurant (top); Rogers Centre (above)

CUTTING-EDGE CULTURE

Check out what's on at the Buddies in Bad Times Theatre (▷ 90), which stages productions that challenge social boundaries.

Explore unconventional works on display at the Museum of Contemporary Canadian Art (▷ 33).

Find out what came top in the annual awards at the Design Exchange (▷ 46–47).

Historic it may be, but the Distillery District (▷ 48–49) has a lively program of non-mainstream shows and events, from the Toronto Alternative Arts and Fashion Week to up-and-coming bands and innovative arts and crafts.

An art exhibition taking place in marquees in the Distillery District (above right); a blues concert attracts an appreciative audience in the Distillery District (right)

Cyclists on the Toronto Islands and a yacht near Centre Island

FRESH AIR AND EXERCISE

Rent a bicycle and pedal around the Toronto Islands (▷ 64–65).

Skim across Lake Ontario in a boat rented from the Harbourfront Centre Sailing and Power-boating (▷ 63).

Take the subway to High Park (▷ 103) and hike through the natural forest of the Spring Creek and West Ravine nature trails.

Have a dip in the lake at The Beaches (▷ 103) or Toronto Islands (▷ 64–65).

Sign up, if you can, for a 'keeper for the day' program at Toronto Zoo (▷ 102); otherwise there's plenty of walking around the spacious enclosures.

INSIDE INFORMATION

Lectures by experts open up new insights at the Royal Ontario Museum (▷ 82–83)

The Ontario Science Centre (▷ 100–101) occasionally hosts presentations by members of the Royal Astronomical Society of Canada.

Head for St. Lawrence Market (▷ 51) any Saturday at noon for demonstrations by food experts, preceded by a short talk about the history of the market (in the South Market building).

Find out what the provincial government is up to by watching parliament in session at the Ontario Legislature (▷ 81).

Ontario Legislature (above); Hanlan's Point (below)

A LAID-BACK AFTERNOON

Linger over a cappuccino and cake at Café Diplomatico (▷ 39) and absorb the atmosphere of Little Italy (▷ 33).

Escape the bustle of Yonge Street and savor the peaceful haven of the Allan Gardens (▷ 52).

Take a picnic to the Toronto Islands (▷ 64–65) and laze away the afternoon on the beach or under a shady tree.

Stretch out on the grass at the peaceful Toronto Music Garden (▷ 66), perhaps soothed by an open-air recital.

GREAT LIVE MUSIC

Check out Massey Hall (▷ 56). Built in 1894, this National Historic Site has had many famous faces appear on its stage, and it continues to be one of Toronto's finest concert venues.

Celebrity connections (Alex Lifeson of Rush) guarantee top-notch rock, jazz, funk and R&B at the Orbit Room (▷ 38).

Known for showcasing future stars from home and abroad, the Horseshoe Tavern (▷ 37) is a Toronto institution.

Chill out to the folk/acoustic performers in the intimate C'Est What cellar bar (▷ 56).

Catch an open-air world music concert on the WestJet Stage at the Harbourfront Centre (▷ 70).

Join the crowds for a megastar concert at the the Rogers Centre (▷ 33).

WINDOW SHOPPING

Browse the dozen traders at Toronto Antiques on King (▷ 36) for treasures that would never fit in a suitcase.

Stroll around chic Yorkville (▷ 86) with its array of upscale designer boutiques—Prada, Chanel, Gucci, et al—and see where the celebrities come to shop.

Toronto has plenty of outlets to hear blues (top) and jazz (above)

Wander along Queen Street West (▷ 32) for cutting-edge Canadian fashion designers as well as international couturiers.

Drool over the superstar designer footwear at John Fluevog (▷ 36).

Yorkville is Toronto's classy shopping area, with plenty of designer names (left and above)

Toronto by Area

DOWNTOWN WEST

DOWNTOWN EAST

LAKESHORE AND ISLANDS

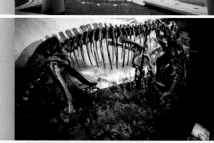

QUEEN'S PARK AND MIDTOWN

FARTHER AFIELD

Downtown West

This area buzzes with creative energy: in the theaters and concert halls of the Entertainment District, in the design houses of the Fashion District and in the art galleries. The CN Tower is an icon of architectural creativity—and you might see sporting creativity in the Rogers Centre.

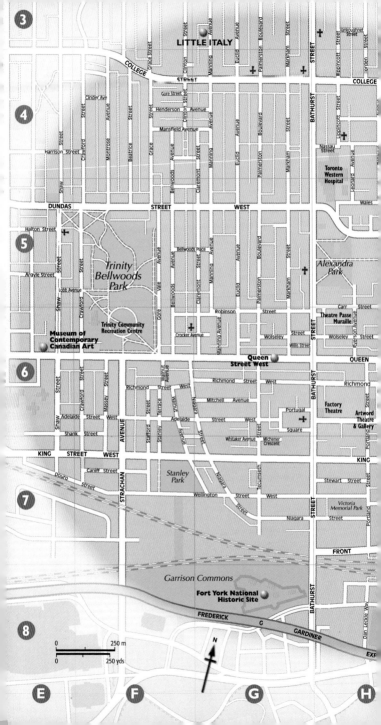

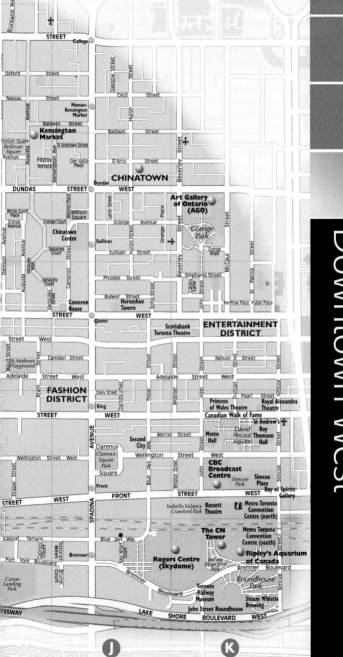

Brunswick Avenue

College

STREET

Oxford Street

Nassau Street

Glasgow Street

Cecil Street

Huron Street

Baldwin Street

Nassau-Kensington Market

Kensington Market

Baldwin Street

D'Arcy Street

Beverley Street

Denison Square
Bellevue Square
Avenue

Fitzroy Terrace

St Andrews Street

Glen Baillie Place

Kensington Ave

Augusta Avenue

CHINATOWN

DUNDAS STREET

Dundas Street WEST

White Court Place

Grange Avenue

Orange Court

Willison Square

Larch Street

Grange Avenue

Grange Place

Art Gallery of Ontario (AGO)

St Patrick Street

Chinatown Centre

Napanee Court

Sullivan

Huron Street

Grange

Grange Park

Grange Road

Denison Avenue

Vanauley Walk

Cameron Street

Sullivan Street

Phoebe Street

Beverley Street

Stephanie Street

McCaul Street

Vanauley Court

Vanauley Street

Cameron House

Bulwer Street

Horseshoe Tavern

Soho Street

Calvert Lane

John Street

Renfrew Place

Pullan Place

STREET WEST

Queen Street

Scotiabank Toronto Theatre

ENTERTAINMENT DISTRICT

Street West

Maud Street

St Andrews Playground

Camden Street

Nelson Street

Adelaide Street West

Adelaide Street West

Brant Street

Charlotte Street

FASHION DISTRICT

Oxley Street

Peter Street

Widmer Street

John Street

Duncan Street

Pearl Street

Simcoe Street

King STREET WEST

Princess of Wales Theatre

Royal Alexandra Theatre

Canadian Walk of Fame

SPADINA AVENUE

Mercer Street

Second City

Metro Hall

David Pecaut Square

St Andrew's

Roy Thomson Hall

Clarence Square

Clarence Square Park

Wellington Street West

Blue Jays Way

Windsor Street

Wellington Street West

CBC Broadcast Centre

Simcoe Park

Simcoe Place

Bay of Spirits Gallery

Draper Street

Front Street

FRONT STREET WEST

Isabella Valancy Crawford Park

Bassett Theatre

Metro Toronto Convention Centre (north)

Iceboat Terrace

Telegram Mews

Portland

Fort York Boulevard

Brunel Court

Blue Jays Way

New Wharf Court

Blue Jays Way

The CN Tower

Bobbie Rosenfeld Park

Metro Toronto Convention Centre (south)

Ripley's Aquarium of Canada

Canoe Landing Park

Bremner

Rogers Centre (Skydome)

Bremner Boulevard

Roundhouse Park

Toronto Railway Museum

Steam Whistle Brewing

SSWAY

LAKE SHORE BOULEVARD WEST

John Street Roundhouse

J

K

Art Gallery of Ontario

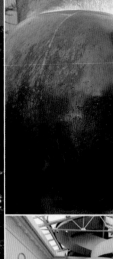

HIGHLIGHTS

- *Corpus* (Bernini)
- *The Massacre of the Innocents* (Rubens)
- *The Fire in the Saint-Jean Quarter, Seen Looking Westward* (Joseph Légaré)
- *West Wind* (Tom Thomson)

TIP

- The AGO restaurant is a cut above the usual museum café. It offers fine dining from a skilled chef, and organic ingredients sourced from sustainable farming.

The Art Gallery of Ontario (AGO), one of North America's finest art galleries, has undergone various expansions over the years, making it one of the largest galleries on the continent; the collections are a sheer joy to behold.

New look The Transformation AGO project was sparked when Kenneth Thomson gifted his collection of some 2,000 works to the gallery, together with funding to help display them. More funds were raised to meet the $276 million cost. Toronto-born Frank Gehry's stunning design includes a soaring 200m (600ft) glass frontage along Dundas street, through which passersby can see into one of the sculpture galleries, a new four-story titanium-and-glass south wing, and major improvements to the existing building.

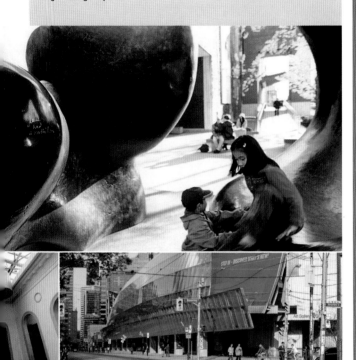

Clockwise from left: Cherub fountain outside the Ontario Art Gallery; children playing among some exhibits; the stunning glass frontage designed by Frank Gehry; interior of the light-filled gallery

Collections The gallery has a total collection of around 80,000 works, covering many periods, genres and parts of the world. It also has a lively schedule of events, educational programs and community projects. The Canadian galleries range from First Nations art to the Group of Seven to innovative contemporary artists. There are also important European works—the 17th-century collection is outstanding—with works by Van Gogh, Picasso, Chagall, Modigliani, Gaugin, the surrealists and many others, while the African and Australian Aboriginal art collection is the finest in North America. The AGO also houses the largest collection of Henry Moore works in the world, with plaster and bronze maquettes. You can hear recordings of Moore discussing his work and his affection for Toronto, and see some of the items that inspired him.

THE BASICS

www.ago.net

✚ K5

✉ 317 Dundas Street West

☎ 416/979-6648

🕐 Tue–Sun 10–5.30 (Wed till 8.30pm)

🍴 Restaurant (tel 416/979-6688), café

🚇 St. Patrick

🚋 505 Dundas streetcar

♿ Very good

💲 Moderate

❓ Tours, lectures, films, concerts

The CN Tower

- Glass Floor
- SkyPod
- EdgeWalk
- The Red Rocket motion theater rides
- The ride up

TIP

- Instead of rushing to the tower in the morning, wait until evening, head for the SkyPod and stay to watch the sun go down and the city lights go on. It's quite a sight.

The CN Tower, 553m (1,815ft) high, is Toronto's trademark building. It was derided at first but ultimately embraced by citizens. Until 2010, the CN Tower was the tallest building in the world, then a hotel in Dubai overtook it on its way to a final height of 829.8m (2,722ft).

On a clear day It's certainly a stomach-churning experience to rocket up at 3m (10ft) per second in glass-fronted elevators to the Look Out level, where there are breathtaking views. Here you can stand—if you dare—on the Glass Floor, 342m (1,122ft) above the ground, then step out onto the outdoor observation deck. On a clear day, you can see the mist of Niagara Falls on the other side of the lake, though the safety netting detracts a little. Take the elevator

Exterior and interior views of the tower, with the café on the observation deck and the view from the SkyPod windows

another 33 stories up to the SkyPod at 447m (1,465ft). The tower has attracted record-seekers—including the multi world-record holder Ashrita Furman, who bounced on his pogo stick up the 1,899 steps to the LookOut roof in 57 minutes and 51 seconds. In 2002 Paralympian athlete Jeff Adams climbed the stairs in a wheelchair, and there have been many other endurance and daredevil feats. An annual stair-climb event attracts thousands of entrants, who raise money for charity.

Shopping and other entertainments Down at the base of the tower there's hands-on action in the Arcade, featuring techno games and simulator rides. The Maple Leaf Cinema shows a 22-minute film on how the tower was built. The Marketplace offers varied shopping.

THE BASICS

www.cntower.ca

+ K8

✉ 301 Front Street West

☎ 416/868-6937

🕐 Tower daily 9am–10.30pm. Other attractions vary

🍴 360 Restaurant, tel 416/362-5411, Horizons, Le Café

Ⓤ Union

🚋 510 Spadina streetcar

♿ Very good

💲 Observation deck expensive; games expensive

Fort York National Historic Site

HIGHLIGHTS

● Officers' Quarters
● Stone Magazine
● Artillery demonstrations

TIP

● Visit during July and August, when well-drilled, uniformed students perform guard drills, artillery demonstrations, military music and drumming.

This complex of buildings, sandwiched between the railroad tracks and the highway, will give you a historic jolt back to 1813 when muddy York was a rough-and-ready imperial outpost.

Toronto's historic birthplace The Fort York National Historic Site is the birthplace of modern urban Toronto and it has the largest collection of 1812-era military structures in the country. As part of an ongoing revitalization project, a new visitor center was opened in late 2014, which has been sensitively designed to blend into the historic site. New exhibits include rarely or never seen before objects, such as war service uniforms and Canadian-made rifles, and contemporary art featuring the war of 1812.

Costumed interpreters and re-created rooms help visitors to imagine life in the fort during the 19th century

Fort York and the White House On April 27, 1813, during the War of 1812, 2,700 Americans stormed ashore from Lake Ontario. They drove out the troops at Fort York and set fire to Government House and the Parliament Buildings. In 1814, in retaliation, the British occupied Washington and burned the president's residence. According to Canadian legend, the Americans covered up the blackened walls with white paint, and from then it was called the White House, but the Americans say it was named for the color of the stone.

Military memorabilia John Graves Simcoe built a garrison on the site of Fort York in 1793. The fort was strengthened in 1811 (the west wall and circular battery date from that time) and, shortly after the events of 1813, the British rebuilt it; most of the fort's buildings date from then.

THE BASICS

www.toronto.ca/culture
www.forkyork.ca

➕ G8

✉ Garrison Road, off Lakeshore Boulevard

☎ 416/392-6907

🕐 Victoria Day–Labour Day daily 10–5; rest of year Mon–Fri 10–4, Sat–Sun 10–5. May be closed for special events

🚋 511 Bathurst streetcar

♿ Few

💷 Inexpensive

❓ Jul–Aug: tours by interpreters in costume

Kensington Market

 TOP 25

Colorful shops and goods for sale at Kensington Market

THE BASICS

www.kensington-market.ca

H5

Bounded by Spadina Avenue and Bathurst Street and College and Dundas streets

Stores 11–7 (food stores open earlier)

505 Dundas or 510 Spadina streetcars

HIGHLIGHTS

- Blue Banana Market
- Global Cheese
- Segovia Meats
- My Market Bakery
- Caribbean Corner
- Casa Acoreana
- Essence of Life Organics

Colorful, quirky, a riot of street sounds and tempting aromas… and yet this is down-to-earth shopping among down-to-earth people. Kensington Market has grown out of a former Jewish enclave into a multiethnic hub where locals congregate and visitors come to enjoy the atmosphere. The federal government declared the market a National Historic Site in 2006.

Tastes of the World Culinary delights are the major draw here, but don't expect to find a central market square—there is just a series of narrow streets with stores selling a colorful array of food. Wander along Kensington and Augusta avenues and Baldwin Street for West Indian grocery stores full of sugar cane, plantains, yucca and the like, and for delicatessens, fresh fish stores and artisan cheeses from around the world. Augusta and Baldwin have health foods aplenty, too.

Street Vibe Food and history aside, there is an edgy, up-to-the-minute feel about the place, with a lot of young fashion designers selling in the market boutiques (▷ Fresh Collective, 35), and individualists combing the stores to create their own look, often with a "vintage" element. There's a café culture here, too, with intellectuals having earnest conversations, people chilling out and visitors lingering over their coffee and drinking in the scene. Some of the cafés and restaurants have live music in the evenings.

Get up close to sharks, rays, jellyfish and a host of marine life

TOP 25

Ripley's Aquarium of Canada

One of Toronto's newest and most popular attractions, Ripley's Aquarium opened to the public in late 2013. Conveniently, it is located right next to the CN Tower.

Freshwater and saltwater This popular aquarium exhibits over 13,500 exotic specimens, from more than 450 species, organized into nine distinct galleries. The Canadian Waters gallery includes the giant Pacific octopus, wolf eels, lobsters, and rockfish. One exhibit, not to be missed,simulates waves, with Pacific kelp calmly flowing through the surges.

The exhibitions The Rainbow Reef shows off the tropical species from the Indo-Pacific region and includes daily interactive dive shows. At the Dangerous Lagoon you'll move through an underwater tunnel while gazing up and around at sharks, stingrays, and the occasional turtle. Hands-on activities are available at the Discovery Centre while the Touch exhibits allow visitors to touch sharks, stingrays, and horseshoe crabs. Mother Nature's Art gallery is home to the world's most delicate species, such as the red lionfish, electric eel, lined seahorse, and weedy sea dragon. The Ray Bay focuses on stingrays, which you can see being fed, while the Shoreline gallery gets you close-up with sharks. Plenty of jellyfish can be seen at the Planet Jellies gallery and the Life Support Systems gallery allows visitors to get a behind-the-scenes look into the aquarium's life-support and filtration equipment.

THE BASICS

www.ripleyaquariums.com

🚉 K8

✉ 288 Bremner Boulevard

☎ 647/351-3474

🕐 Daily 9am-11pm

🍴 Ripley's Cafe

🚋 510 Spadina streetcar

♿ Good

💲 Expensive

HIGHLIGHTS

● Spotting the Giant Pacific Octopus
● Close-ups with sharks and stingrays
● Dangerous Lagoon underwater tunnel

TIP

Purchase tickets online in advance of your visit to avoid long lines.

DOWNTOWN WEST TOP 25

Queen Street West

The historic red-brick frontages (left); sculptures in Nathan Phillips Square (right)

THE BASICS

➕ J6

✉ Queen Street West between Bathurst and Simcoe

🍴 Restaurants, cafés and snackbars

🚌 501 Queen streetcar

HIGHLIGHTS

● Queen Mother Cafe
● Scouting out vintage clothing treasures
● Celebrity spotting

Set against a backdrop of gorgeous historic buildings, the Queen Street West neighborhood is one of the trendiest shopping and dining areas in Toronto.

Hip haven Queen Street West runs along its namesake Queen Street, between Bathurst and Simcoe, and during the 1960s and 1970s, it was well known as a hippy hangout with cheap rent and greasy spoon diners. During the 1980s it became the defacto nightclub strip and the music scene quickly churned out famous punk rockers and gave rise to the popular MuchMusic channel.

Arty crowd Soon after, the students from the nearby Ontario College of Art & Design (now called OCAD University) began to transform the Queen Street West neighborhood into a vibrant arts community. This popularized the area, increasing the living costs, and eventually changing it from a hippy hangout to the haven it is today.

Toronto's Fashion District The area is now home to eager young designers, and an extensive array of shoe, fabric, bead, and clothing stores borders Queen Street West to the north, while the west of Queen Street West is dubbed gallery central. All along Queen Street you'll find patio-fronted cafes, trendy bars, excellent live music venues, fine-dining restaurants, and the occasional diner too.

More to See

CBC BROADCAST CENTRE

www.cbc.ca

This distinctive work of architecture with a colorful exterior is one of the largest broadcasting centers in North America. In the grand Barbara Frum Atrium, named for the distinguished Canadian journalist and designed by Philip Johnson, you can see radio hosts speaking into microphones and technicians keeping everyone on track. The space is 10 floors high and topped with a skylight. The little museum (capacity 50 people) is fun and free. Enjoy a variety of clips from radio and TV, and the interactive exhibits. Special exhibitions have included radio sound effects and props from popular kids' programs.

➕ K7 ✉ 250 Front Street West ☎ 416/205-5574 🕐 Mon–Fri 9–5 🍴 Cafeteria Ⓤ Union ♿ Good

CHINATOWN

Sprawling along Dundas and Spadina, the original Chinatown bustles day and night. People shop for green mustard and bok choy, fresh crabs and live fish, and herbal stores selling "relaxing tea" and ginseng that costs hundreds of dollars for just one ounce. Restaurants are a big part of the attraction, while Chinese New Year, with dragon dances and drumming, is a highlight of the Toronto calendar.

➕ J5 ✉ St. Patrick 🚋 505 Dundas streetcar

LITTLE ITALY

http://littleitalycollegest.com

A vibrant Italian community thrives along College Street between Euclid and Shaw, where the street lamps bear neon maps of Italy. Old-style cafés with coffee machines operate alongside more modern, fashionable establishments. At night, in particular, the area buzzes with energy as people flock to the authentic restaurants.

➕ G3 🚋 506 Carlton streetcar

MUSEUM OF CONTEMPORARY CANADIAN ART

www.mocca.ca

Founded in 1999, the Museum of Contemporary Canadian Art (MOCCA) presents works by established and up-and-coming Canadian artists. The permanent collection has more than 400 works by about 150 artists, including Stephen Andrews, Ivan Eyre, Harold Klunder, and Shelagh Keeley. In addition, there are works in other media, such as video, installation, photography, and performance.

➕ E6 ✉ 952 Queen Street West at Shaw ☎ 416/395-0067 🕐 Tue–Sun 11–6 🚋 501 Queen streetcar ♿ Good ✋ Free

ROGERS CENTRE

www.rogerscentre.com

One of the largest Major League baseball stadiums ever built, a tour at the home of the Blue Jays can be fascinating. The stadium incorporates an 11-story hotel where the rooms have great views facing onto the field and can be rented on game nights for upward of $300. The Toronto Argonauts (Canadian Football League) also play here; other entertainment includes circuses to concerts and ice shows.

➕ K8 ✉ 1 Blue Jays Way ☎ 416/341-1000 🕐 Times vary, call ahead Ⓤ Union ♿ Good ✋ Tours moderate

Downtown West Highlights

Start with the city's best view, then tour theaterland and a couple of colorful neighborhoods, with the superb AGO along the way.

DISTANCE: 3km (1.8 miles)　**ALLOW:** 2.5 hours

DOWNTOWN WEST WALK

START

THE CN TOWER
K8　510 Spadina streetcar

END

KENSINGTON MARKET
H5　505 Dundas streetcar

❶ Walk east from The CN Tower along Front Street to check out the lobby-studios and museum of the CBC Broadcast Centre.

❽ Cross to the west side of Spadina and find Baldwin Street. Go down Baldwin Street into the heart of Kensington Market.

❷ Backtrack, then turn right up John Street to King Street.

❼ Exit the AGO on Dundas and go left through Chinatown, turning right on Spadina to explore more of this colorful neighborhood.

❸ Turn right to see the Frank Stella murals in the Princess of Wales Theatre, then cross over to walk along the Canadian Walk of Fame, with Roy Thomson Hall to your right and the Royal Alexandra Theatre opposite.

❻ Turn right on John Street and walk north to enter Grange Park and the Art Gallery of Ontario.

❹ Turn left and walk up Simcoe Street, bordering the Entertainment District, to Queen Street West.

❺ Go left on Queen West to the junction with John Street, and stop at the corner to peek into CTV's street-level studio to see who's on.

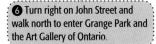

Shopping

ABRAHAM'S

This may not qualify as a high-end antiques store, but it is certainly a cherry-picker's delight. The space is jammed to the ceiling with all kinds of curios and ephemera, from gas pumps to bicycles and neon beer signs to musical instruments.

➕ H6 ✉ 635 Queen Street West ☎ 416/504-6210
🚋 501 Queen streetcar

ANNE SPORTUN JEWELLERY

Designer Anne Sportun uses traditional gold-smithing techniques to make striking pieces inspired by nature and the universal language of shape and symbol. Richly colored precious stones are set in rings, earrings, necklaces or pendants. She will custom-make design as well.

➕ F7 ✉ 742 Queen Street West ☎ 416/363-4114
🚋 501 Queen streetcar

BOOKHOU

www.bookhou.com
A local husband-and-wife design team create beautiful bags, pillow covers, children's clothing, pottery, and furniture. They beautifully and esthetically incorporate natural materials such as linen, felt, canvas, clay, and wood.

➕ G5 ✉ 798 Dundas Street West ☎ 416/7203-2549
🚋 505 Dundas streetcar

CABARET

The place to buy wonderful period costumes and retro fashions. Seek out velvet and sequined gowns or that perfect smoking jacket.

➕ G6 ✉ 672 Queen Street West (west of Palmerston) ☎ 416/504-7126
🚋 Osgoode 🚋 501 Queen streetcar

CLUB MONACO

For casual, young fashions there is nowhere better than this chain, with several outlets in the city. This is the brand's flagship store.

➕ H6 ✉ 403 Queen Street West ☎ 416/979-5633
🚋 Queen Street West streetcar

DRAKE GENERAL STORE

Located inside the Drake Hotel, this funky shop sells intriguing curios and souvenirs that are perfectly Canadian. Find local retro maps, Toronto-based Camp Skincare products, housemade teas, and a host of other gift ideas here.

➕ D6 ✉ 1144 Queen Street West ☎ 416/531-5042
🚋 501 Queen streetcar

ESP (ERIN STUMP PROJECTS)

www.erinstumpprojects.com
Bright little art gallery in the Dundas West neighborhood that features mostly the work of up-and-coming artists from the Toronto area.

➕ D4 ✉ 1450 Dundas Street West ☎ 647/345-6163
🚋 505 Dundas streetcar

FREDA'S

Canadian designer Freda Iordanous dresses TV personalities and actresses, and all her casual, business and evening garments for women (in sizes 4 to 20) are produced on the premises. Lines from Europe are also stocked.

➕ G7 ✉ 86 Bathurst Street ☎ 416/703-0304 or 1-888/373-3271 🚋 511 Bathurst or 504 King streetcars

FRESH COLLECTIVE

www.freshcollective.com
Kensington Market clothing and accessory store with an original flair featuring local designers and unique international labels.

➕ H5 ✉ 274 Augusta Avenue ☎ 416/966-0123
🚋 505 Dundas streetcar

FROM HOCKEY TO HOLLYWOOD

www.fromhockeytohollywood.com
Sports fans head here to purchase the shirt, hat or signed gear of their favorite team or player.

➕ K7 ✉ 322A King Street West ☎ 416/971-8848
🚋 St. Andrew

GOTSTYLE

A cool place in the Fashion District for modern menswear, with designer brands, independent labels,

DOWNTOWN WEST ENTERTAINMENT AND NIGHTLIFE

accessories, and shoes. There's a vintage barber shop too.

🚹 G7 ✉ 62 Bathurst Street ☎ 416/260-9696 🚋 504 King or 511 Bathurst streetcars

JOHN FLUEVOG

www.fluevog.com

The most flamboyant shoes imaginable are found at this ultrahip outlet. Madonna and Paula Abdul have both been known to shop in this store.

🚹 K6 ✉ 242 Queen Street West ☎ 416/581-1420 🚇 Osgoode 🚋 501 Queen streetcar

LAVISH & SQUALOR

www.lavishandsqualor.com

Independent hipster haven with unique clothing labels and accessories for sale, plus there's an espresso bar and art gallery.

🚹 K6 ✉ 253 Queen Street West ☎ 416/599-4779 🚋 501 Queen streetcar

THE MONKEY'S PAW

Antiquarian shop specializing in rare, eclectic books. There's also a Biblio-mat machine that dispenses a random secondhand book for $2.

🚹 E5 ✉ 1229 Dundas Street West ☎ 416/531-2123 🚋 505 Dundas streetcar

MOUNTAIN EQUIPMENT CO-OP (MEC)

www.mec.ca

Even if you're not a climber, you'll find a great range of outdoor clothing, footwear and camping gear here. The store's roof is a sustainable re-creation of a prairie environment and the store takes in old batteries for recycling.

🚹 J7 ✉ 400 King Street West ☎ 416/340-2667 🚋 504 King Street West or 510 Spadina streetcars

THE POWER PLANT

www.thepowerplant.org

Devoted to contemporary art by Canadian and international artists, this thought-provoking gallery is housed in a 1920s brick powerhouse at the Harbourfront, with the

towering smokestack still in place.

🚹 K9 ✉ 231 Queens Quay West ☎ 416/7973-4949 🚋 509 Harbourfront streetcar

SONIC BOOM

www.sonicboommusic.com

The definitive place for vinyl, new and used. Find a large collection of CDs, plus collectible VHS and even old cassette tapes here too.

🚹 G2 ✉ 782 Bathurst Street ☎ 416/532-0334 🚋 511 Bathurst streetcar

TEN REN TEA

www.tenrentea.com

In the heart of Chinatown, this store stocks an excellent range of fine teas in urns and also sells health-oriented infusions and slimming tea. You will also find a superb stock of tiny Chinese teapots and teacups in a range of patterns and colors.

🚹 J5 ✉ 454 Dundas Street West at Huron ☎ 416/598-7872 🚋 505 Dundas streetcar

TORONTO ANTIQUES ON KING

High-quality dealers, who are well known in their specialties, operate the dozen booths here. Shoppers will find estate jewelry, maps and prints, porcelain, silver, Oriental rugs, scientific instruments and much more.

🚹 K7 ✉ 284 King Street West at Duncan ☎ 416/260-9057 🚇 St. Andrew

---

BOOKSTORES GALORE

Toronto's bookstore scene has dramatically dwindled over the last decade, but while some of the larger chains, including Chapters/Indigo, continue to close up stores, smaller, independent booksellers are beginning to thrive once again. Local independents include the elegant **Ben McNally Books** (▷ 55), offering fewer mainstream choices, **The Beguiling Books & Art** (🚹 G2 ✉ 601 Markham Street ☎ 416/533-9168, www.beguilingbooksandart.com) and **Book City**, with four stores: Yonge Street, Danforth Avenue, Queen Street East, and Bloor Street West.

Entertainment and Nightlife

BARHOP
www.barhopbar.com
A fantastic beer bar serving 36 craft beers on tap and over 100 bottled and canned varieties. The good modern menu focuses on comfort foods. Enjoy people watching from the street-side patio.
🚩 J7 ✉ 319 King Street West ☎ 647/352-7476 🚃 504 King streetcar

BAR ITALIA
www.bar-italia.ca
This slick spot in Little Italy is favored by the young and beautiful. Upstairs there's a plush lounge area for chilling. Downstairs it's coffee, alcohol and Italian specialties all round.
🚩 G4 ✉ 582 College Street ☎ 416/535-3621 🚃 506 Carlton streetcar

BAR +
www.bar-plus.com
Bar and karaoke lounge with private rooms that can seat up to 25 people. Modern decor, bottle service, and an app for your smartphone so you'll always have the most up-to-date songs ready to belt out.
🚩 M5 ✉ 360 Yonge Street ☎ 416/340-7154 🚃 505 Dundas streetcar

EL CONVENTO RICO
www.elconventorico.com
Famed for its weekend 1am drag shows. Lambada the night away until 4am.

🚩 F3 ✉ 750 College Street at Crawford ☎ 416/588-7800 🚃 506 Carlton streetcar

CROCODILE ROCK
www.crocrock.ca
Bar-restaurant and dance space with a pool lounge. The crowd grooves to 70s and 80s dance sounds.
🚩 K6 ✉ 240 Adelaide Street West at Duncan ☎ 416/599-9751 🚇 St. Andrew

DRAKE HOTEL BAR
www.thedrakehotel.ca
In an artsy hotel there's an eclectic program of live music and DJs. Offerings include soul, funk, reggae, jazz, opera and French *chanson*.
🚩 D6 ✉ 1150 Queen Street West ☎ 416/531-5042 🚃 501 Queen streetcar

THE ELGIN AND WINTER GARDEN THEATRE CENTRE
Owned and run by the Ontario Heritage Trust,

TICKETS & INFORMATION
Get tickets, including day-of-performance half-price admission, at the TO Tix booth at Yonge-Dundas Square (🚩 M5 🚇 Tue–Sat 12–6.30 ☎ 416/536-6468, www.totix.ca). To find out what's on, try *Toronto Life*, *Where Toronto* and the weekend editions of the *Globe & Mail*, *Toronto Star* and *Toronto Sun*. *Now* covers the hip scene, and *Xtra!* gay scene in the city.

these last surviving Edwardian stacked theatres in the world perform shows that are opulent and highly memorable.
🚩 M6 ✉ 189 Yonge Street ☎ 416/314-2901 🚇 Queen

FACTORY THEATRE
www.factorytheatre.ca
This theater is dedicated to producing the works of new Canadianplaywrights, which are put on in two theaters. Many of the company's productions have been on international tours.
🚩 H6 ✉ 125 Bathurst ☎ 416/504-9971 🚃 511 Bathurst streetcar

THE FIFTH
www.thefifth.com
An older crowd (and sometimes visiting celebrities) gathers in the loft-like space. The music leans to lounge and allows for conversation.
🚩 K6 ✉ 225 Richmond Street West ☎ 416/979-3000 🚇 Osgoode

HORSESHOE TAVERN
www.horseshoetavern.com
Established in 1947, this is the place where The Police, The Band, Blue Rodeo and Barenaked Ladies got their start in Canada.
🚩 J6 ✉ 370 Queen Street West ☎ 416/598-4226 🚃 501 Queen streetcar

NORTHWOOD
www.northwoodto.ca
Cafe by day, bar by night, this Victorian/industrial-

DOWNTOWN WEST ENTERTAINMENT AND NIGHTLIFE

designed space focuses on local craft breweries, Ontario wines, and a Canadiana-inspired liquor selection.

🚇 F2 ✉ 815 Bloor Street West ☎ 416/846-8324
🚊 Ossington

ORBIT ROOM
www.orbitroom.ca
Co-founded by Alex Lifeson of Rush, this continues to be a premier venue for live R&B, funk, alternative rock and jazz.

🚇 G4 ✉ 580A College Street ☎ 416/535-0613
🚊 506 Carlton streetcar

PRINCESS OF WALES THEATRE
www.mirvish.com
Opened in 1993, this 2,000-seat theater has one of the largest stages in North America and clever three-level seating giving excellent sight-lines. The acoustics are near perfect and the craftsmanship is superb—the murals alone are worth a visit.

🚇 K7 ✉ King Street West at John Street ☎ 416/872-1212, 1-800/461-3333 tickets
🚊 504 King streetcar

REX HOTEL JAZZ AND BLUES BAR
www.therex.ca
This club offers top local and up-and-coming modern jazz artists, and a great night out.

🚇 K6 ✉ 194 Queen Street West ☎ 416/598-2475
🚊 501 Queen streetcar

RIVOLI
www.rivoli.ca
Hip club-restaurant for an eclectic mix of grunge, blues, rock, jazz, indie and comedy.

🚇 J6 ✉ 334 Queen Street West ☎ 416/596-1908
🚊 Osgoode 🚊 501 Queen streetcar

ROYAL ALEXANDRA THEATRE
www.mirvish.com
The century-old theater has been played by many of the all-time greats of the stage, including John Gielgud, Orson Welles, Fred Astaire, and the Marx Brothers. The interior remains the epitome of a 19th-century theater.

🚇 K7 ✉ King Street West at Duncan ☎ 416/872-1212, 1-800/461-3333 tickets, 416/593-0351 admin 🚊 504 King streetcar

Two Toronto institutions perform principally at Roy Thomson Hall. The Toronto Symphony is the city's premier orchestra. In addition to its classical repertoire, it plays light popular music and its outdoor summer concerts are well supported. The Toronto Mendelssohn Choir performs great choral works, and is noted for Handel's *Messiah*. The choir performed on the soundtrack of the movie *Schindler's List*.

ROY THOMSON HALL
www.roythomson.com
This is the foremost concert hall in Canada. The greatest international orchestras and classical performers play here, with occasional world culture and other genres. Check the website for details of forthcoming events and performances.

🚇 K7 ✉ 60 Simcoe Street
☎ 416/872-4255 box office
🚊 504 King streetcar

SECOND CITY
www.secondcity.com
This venue is the source of many well-known Canadian comedians who have made it big internationally—Mike Myers, John Candy, Dan Aykroyd, Bill Murray, Martin Short, and others, so it's the place to spot new talent.

🚇 J7 ✉ 51 Mercer Street
☎ 416/343-0011 🚊 504 King streetcar

THEATRE PASSE MURAILLE
www.passemuraille.ca
This is another theater company that nurtures contemporary Canadian playwrights. It produces an excellent program of innovative and provocative works by such figures as Daniel David Moses and Wajdi Mouawad. There are two stages, one catering to an audience of 185, the other for just 55.

🚇 H6 ✉ 16 Ryerson Avenue
☎ 416/504-7529 🚊 501 Queen streetcar

Restaurants

PRICES

Prices are approximate, based on a 3-course meal for one person.

$$$$	over $80
$$$	$60–$80
$$	$35–$60
$	under $35

360 AT THE CN TOWER ($$$$)

www.cntower.ca
Don't write this revolving restaurant off as a tourist trap. It is, in fact, a fine-dining experience, with an extensive à la carte menu of impressive dishes that make the best use of Canadian produce, including prime beef, Atlantic salmon and lobster, and Ontario pickerel. Superb wine list.

🚇 K8 ✉ 301 Front Street West ☎ 416/362-5411 🕐 Lunch and dinner daily 🚈 Union

BAR ITALIA ($$)

www.bar-italia.ca
Italian chic with an upstairs pool hall and a downstairs café jammed at night with a young, buzzing crowd.

🚇 F4 ✉ 582 College Street ☎ 416/535-3621 🕐 Mon–Thu 11am–1am, Fri 11am–2am, Sat 10am–2am, Sun 10am–midnight 🚈 506 Carlton streetcar

CAFÉ DIPLOMATICO ($)

www.cafediplomatico.ca
Still not gussied up, Diplomatico has mosaic marble floors, wrought-iron chairs and a glorious cappuccino machine. A Toronto tradition on weekends.

🚇 G4 ✉ 594 College Street ☎ 416/534-4637 🕐 Sun–Thu 8am–1am, Fri, Sat 8am–2am 🚈 506 Carlton streetcar

CHIADO ($$$)

www.chiadorestaurant.com
Reminiscent of a Lisbon bistro. Stick to such signature Portuguese dishes as the marinated sardines, poached salted cod and the natas do céu.

🚇 E3 ✉ 864 College Street, at Concord Avenue ☎ 416/538-1910 🕐 Lunch Mon–Fri, dinner daily 🚈 506 Carlton streetcar

CRUSH ($$)

www.crushwinebar.com
This handsome ware-house with an open kitchen is not just a wine bar. It serves well-cooked contemporary main and small plates, including tasty game and innovative vegetarian dishes.

🚇 J7 ✉ 455 King Street West at Spadina ☎ 416/977-1234 🕐 Lunch Mon–Fri, dinner daily 🚈 504 King streetcar

A FEW TIPS

Restaurant checks (bills) include a 13 percent harmonized sales tax (HST), though prepared food and beverages under $4 are tax-exempt. Always tip on the pretax total of the check. All restaurants are smoke-free. Call first if this is important to you. Well-dressed casual is acceptable in most restaurants. Men might feel more comfortable wearing a jacket in the more upscale dining spots.

DUMPLING HOUSE RESTAURANT ($)

One of Toronto's best dumpling houses right in the middle of Chinatown—fast service and cheap prices. Watch as the cooks hand roll the dough and fill those little tasty morsels with pork and chives—their most popular dumpling.

🚇 J5 ✉ 328 Spadina Avenue ☎ 416/596-8898 🕐 Daily 11am–11pm 🚈 505 Dundas streetcar

EMA-TEI ($$)

Frequented by many Japanese visitors to Toronto because it delivers absolutely authentic cuisine, from the perfect appetizers to the fresh sushi.

🚇 K6 ✉ 30 St. Patrick Street ☎ 416/340-0472 🕐 Lunch Mon–Fri, dinner daily 🚈 Osgoode

FRANK'S KITCHEN ($$$)

Casual fine dining in a cozy setting. Try the legendary oysters Rockefeller, the crispy gnocchi with Gorgonzola, or the divine housemade truffles.

🔲 G4 ✉ 588 College Street
☎ 416/516-5861 ⏰ Tue–Sun
6pm–10.30pm, closed Mon
🚋 506 Carlton streetcar

FRED'S NOT HERE ($$)

www.fredsnothere.com
A huge, glowing mural
and an open kitchen
share the limelight with
a long, eclectic menu
of interesting dishes.
Mediterranean and
Oriental influences are
in evidence alongside
comfort food such as
slow-roasted beef brisket
or two-way-pork with
roasted crispy pork belly
and bbq pork back ribs.
🔲 K6 ✉ 321 King Street
West ☎ 416/971-9155
⏰ Lunch Tue–Sat 11.30am–
10pm, dinner daily 🚋 504
King streetcar

FUSARO'S ITALIAN KITCHEN ($$)

www.fusaros.com
Authentic southern
Italian eatery that gets
line ups out the door
during the lunch hour.
Try the delcious paninis
for under $10. Casual
patio seating for perfect
people watching.
🔲 J6 ✉ 147 Spadina
Avenue ☎ 416/260-8414
⏰ Mon–Fri 9–9, Sat 11–6.
Closed Sun 🚋 501 Queen
streetcar

THE HARBORD ROOM ($$)

www.theharbordroom.com
This wonderfully inti-
mate gastropub follows
the latest foodie trends

with locally procured
ingredients. Try the
ricotta donuts with spiced
chocolate for dessert.
Making a reservations is
recommended.
🔲 J3 ✉ 89 Harbord Street
☎ 416/962-8989 ⏰ Dinner
daily 5.30pm–2am 🚋 510
Spadina streetcar

MATAHARI ($)

www.mataharigrill.com
Coconut-scented curries,
really fresh fish enhanced
by sauces spiced with
lime leaf, chilis and red
onion, spring rolls and
satays, all served in a
halogen-lit setting.
🔲 J4 ✉ 39 Baldwin Street
(off Spadina) ☎ 416/596-
2832 ⏰ Lunch Mon–Fri, dinner Mon–Sat 🚇 St. Patrick

LE SÉLECT BISTRO ($–$$)

www.leselect.com
Select is as French as
they come, from the

TABLES WITH A VIEW

On the 54th floor of Mies
van der Rohe's TD Bank
Tower, **Canoe** offers a view
of surrounding skyscrapers.
At the top of the Park Hyatt,
the **Roof Lounge** (✉ 4
Avenue Road ☎ 416/925-
1234) affords great views of
downtown. **Scaramouche**
(✉ 1 Benvenuto Place
☎ 416/961-8011) has win-
dow seats on the downtown
skyline. The most stunning
view of all is from **360** on top
of the CN Tower (▷ 39).

pied-de-cochon to the
background jazz. The
weekend brunch is huge-
ly popular so it's worth
making a reservation.
🔲 H7 ✉ 432 Wellington
Street West ☎ 416/596-6405
⏰ Mon–Wed 11.30–11, Thu–
Fri 11.30–11.30, Sat 11am–
midnight, Sun 10.30–10.30
🚋 504 King streetcar

SENSES ($$$)

www.senses.ca
Sophisticated, clean lines
are the hallmark of this
40-seat restaurant in
one of the city's
most luxurious hotels.
Signature dishes include
triple searing of meats
and pan-roasted fish
in a truffle and soya
vinaigrette; and the
desserts are to die for.
🔲 J7 ✉ SoHo Metropolitan
Hotel, 328 Wellington Street
West ☎ 416/935-0400
⏰ Breakfast, lunch and dinner
daily 🚇 Union 🚋 504 King
streetcar

WAH SING ($)

www.wahsing.ca
A mealtime hotspot pop-
ular with locals and tour-
ists alike, where the seafood tank is often filled
with giant queen crabs
ready to sizzle with ginger
and onion. Also worth
looking out for are the
deep-fried oysters, duck
with Peking sauce and, in
season, two lobsters for
the price of one.
🔲 K4 ✉ 47 Baldwin Street
☎ 416/599-8822 ⏰ Daily
11.30–11 🚋 505 Dundas
streetcar

This is the financial, commercial and administrative heart of the city. But there's entertainment, historic sights, and hockey heroes at the Air Canada Centre and Hockey Hall of Fame. Much of the PATH underground city is beneath these streets.

Sights	44–53
Walk	54
Shopping	55
Entertainment and Nightlife	56
Restaurants	57–58

Top 25	TOP 25
City Hall ▷ 44	
Design Exchange ▷ 46	
Distillery Historic District ▷ 48	
Hockey Hall of Fame ▷ 50	
St. Lawrence Market ▷ 51	

STREET

Allan Gardens
Greenhouse

GARDEN DISTRICT

Gerrard Street East

Sherbourne Street

Seaton Street

Ontario Street

George Street

EAST

Pembroke Street

DUNDAS STREET

Oak Street

Cole Street

REGENT PARK EAST

Coatsworth Street

Seaton

Ontario Street

Milan Street

Berkeley Street

Poulett Street

PARLIAMENT STREET

Arnold Avenue

Regent Street

St Bartholomew St

Pashler Avenue

Daniels Spectrum

Sutton Avenue

Sackville Green

Sackville St

Street

Shuter Street

Shuter Street

Moss Park
MOSS PARK

EAST

Britain Street

Stonecutters Lane

Brigden Place

Ontario Street

Richmond Street East

QUEEN STREET EAST

✝ St Paul's Church

Bright Street

Toronto's First Post Office

TOWN OF YORK

✝ **CORKTOWN**

Power Street

KING STREET EAST

Sackville Street

OLD TOWN HERITAGE AREA

Adelaide Street

Alumnae Theatre

DESIGN DISTRICT

East

Berkeley

✝ Little Trinity Anglican

Trinity Street

EASTERN AVENUE

CORKTOWN HERITAGE DISTRICT

George Street

EAST

Princess Street

FRONT STREET EAST

Imperial Oil Opera
Berkeley Street Theatre

PARLIAMENT STREET

GOODERHAM & WORTS

Trinity Street

Cherry Street

Lenox Place

ST LAWRENCE

Wilton Street

Lower Sherbourne Street

The Esplanade
David Crombie Park
Scadding Avenue

Princess Street Park

Princess

Hahn Place

Parliament Square

Mill Street

DISTILLERY HISTORIC DISTRICT

Gooderham & Worts

The Cannery Theatre

Albert Franco Place
Henry Lane Terrace
Frederick

P

Q

City Hall

HIGHLIGHTS

- Council Chamber
- Hall of Memory
- Nathan Phillips Square
- *Metropolis*
- Henry Moore's *Three Way Piece Number Two* ("The Archer")
- Peace Garden
- Reflecting pool
- Podium Green Roof

TIP

- Guided tours are only available to groups, but the website has a good down-loadable self-guiding tour.

Remarkable for its striking design, which shook up Toronto in the early 1960s, City Hall could be a space station, with the council chamber a flying saucer cradled between two semicircular control towers.

Viljo Revell and Nathan Phillips When Mayor Nathan Phillips persuaded the City Council to hold a competition to design a new city hall, the councillors received 520 submissions from 42 countries. Finnish architect Viljo Revell won, and his building opened in 1965. The square in front serves as a site for entertainment; the reflecting pool, where workers eat sandwiches in summer, turns into a skating rink in winter. To the east of City Hall, the Peace Garden contains an eternal flame lit by Pope John Paul II using a flame from the Memorial for Peace

Clockwise from left: City Hall with the old town hall clock tower; nighttime view from above; the Peace Garden; Henry Moore's sculpture The Archer; *daytime view of City Hall from below*

at Hiroshima. Near the entrance stands Henry Moore's *Three Way Piece Number Two*, affectionately called "The Archer" by Torontonians.

Municipal art City Hall itself contains several artworks. Just inside the entrance, the mural *Metropolis*, by local artist David Partridge, is created from more than 100,000 nails. Continue into the Rotunda and the Hall of Memory, shaped like a sunken amphitheater, where, in the Golden Book of Remembrance, are listed 3,500 Torontonians who died in World War II. At its center rises a large white column supporting the Council Chamber above. The north corridor is lined with a copper-and-glass mosaic called *Views to the City*, depicting historic panoramic views of the city skyline. From here you can take an elevator up to the Council Chamber.

THE BASICS

www.toronto.ca
➕ L6
✉ 100 Queen Street West
☎ 416/338-0338
🕐 Mon–Fri 8.30–4.30
🍴 Cafeteria
🚇 Queen or Osgoode
♿ Very good
💲 Free
❓ Self-guided tour

Design Exchange

HIGHLIGHTS

● The frieze on the facade
● Murals by Charles Comfort
● The staircase
● Canadian Industrial Design collection

TIPS

● Try to catch one of the "Power Lecture" talks, by world-renowned designers.
● The gift shop, not surprisingly, has better-designed goods than most.

Housed in the former Stock Exchange—a splendid Moderne building with its architectural features preserved—the Design Exchange was established in the 1980s to promote Canadian design and to encourage more appreciation of applied arts.

The building In 1986 the city council was persuaded that a design center would be a good idea, but it wasn't until 1994 that it held its official opening in the fine heritage building recently vacated by the Toronto Stock Exchange. Now encased by the TD Centre, the pink granite and limestone facade stands out against the surrounding black-and-glass structure—a frame that serves to emphasize the symmetry of the early 20th-century design. Inside is equally impressive, with some remarkable murals and a fine staircase.

Clockwise from left: the exterior of the building; northeast view of the trading floor of the old Stock Exchange; staircase of the trading floor; murals

The exhibits No other museum in Canada has a collection that is so focused on the preservation of the nation's modern industrial design. The permanent collection includes more than 150 items of furniture, graphic design, industrial design, homewares, decorative arts, sporting goods and other themes. It's fun to look back over the past 70 years of chair design and to see the first item acquired by the Design Exchange—the stylish but bulky Project G2 Stereo. The DX stages exhibitions every year to highlight aspects of design, in the Chalmers Design Centre and Teknion Lounge at ground level and in the 3rd-floor Exhibition Hall. Recent exhibitions have included themes on toy design, a retrospective on French lingerie, Spanish tapas design techniques, and the making of haute couture labels. A highlight of the year is the Design Exchange Awards.

THE BASICS

www.dx.org

🚇 L7

✉ 234 Bay Street

☎ 416/363-6121

🕐 Mon–Sat 10–5

🍴 Restaurants, café and food hall in TD Centre

🚇 King or Union

🚃 504 King streetcar

♿ Very good

💷 Inexpensive

❓ Tours Mon–Fri 2pm

Distillery Historic District

HIGHLIGHTS

● Wandering the cobbled streets between historic buildings
● Distillery Walking Tour and Segway tours
● Glass artists at work in the Tank studio
● Julie M. Gallery
● Corkin Gallery
● Mill Street Brewery tour

TIP

● Movie, TV and music video filming might occasionally block off some areas. On the plus side, you might spot some famous actors and singers.

Vibrant, artsy and atmospheric, a place to shop for artisan crafts and original art, a venue for live music and festivals: It is indeed a far cry from the rundown, deserted former distillery that until recently covered this out-of-the-way site.

Where it began William Gooderham's and James Worts' waterfront distillery started up in 1837, and in just 10 years it had become the world's largest distillery. In 1987, this outstanding example of Victorian industrial design was acquired by Allied Lyons, who spent $25 million on its preservation.

Everything old is new In December 2001, local visionary developers purchased the 13-acre (5ha) site and set about installing new life. Original concrete floors, brick walls and beamed ceilings

Clockwise from left: Balzacs, Coffee Roasters; Trinity Street at night; an aerial view of Trinity Street; Tank House Lane

remain unchanged. More than 340,000 old bricks from Cleveland have been laid in the lanes and alleyways, and a contemporary, creative group of tenants now inhabit the atmospheric buildings.

Arts and culture A jazz festival marked the opening in May 2003 and about 30 festivals still take place each year. Original distillery buildings now house a microbrewery making Ontario's first organic beer, art galleries, nearly 20 artists' studios and lots of interesting stores and boutiques. Goods range from clothing and jewelry to furniture. The performing arts have a large presence, including theater and dance companies and performance schools. The Young Centre for the Performing Arts, with partners George Brown College and Soulpepper Theatre, occupy a complex that includes four performing spaces.

THE BASICS

www.thedistillerydistrict. com

🚇 Q7

✉ Between Mill Street, Parliament Street and Cherry Street

☎ 416/364-1177

🕐 Site opens 10am; stores and galleries, hours vary

🍴 Many outlets

🚉 Union then 72 Pape or 65A Parliament bus

🚋 504 King streetcar to Parliament Street, then walk south

♿ Good

🖐 Free; tours moderate

❓ Various tours

Hockey Hall of Fame

Exhibits (left); replica of the Stanley Cup (right)

THE BASICS

www.hhof.com

+ M7

✉ Brookfield Place at 30 Yonge Street

☎ 416/360-7765

🕐 Late Jun–early Sep and Mar break Mon–Sat 9.30–6, Sun 10–6; Sep–May Mon–Fri 10–5, Sat 9.30–6, Sun 10.30–5

🚇 King or Union Station

🚋 504 King streetcar

♿ Very good

💰 Moderate

HIGHLIGHTS

● Stanley Cup
● NHLPA Game Time
● Montréal Canadiens' dressing room
● EA Sports NHL Slapshot Zone
● The Stanley Cup Odyssey

There's a Canadian saying: First you walk, then you skate. Hockey is to Canadians what football is to the Americans. It's the one game that most Canadians want to watch and take part in.

The Stanley Cup and Hall of Fame The jewel of the museum is the Esso Great Hall, once the grand banking hall of the Bank of Montreal. Here the Stanley Cup, North America's oldest professional sports trophy, is displayed in front of the Honoured Members Wall.

Live action At the Be a Player Zone you will find live shooting booths with sticks and a pail full of pucks; or you can test your skills against goalkeeper Ed Belfour on a life-size computer simulation; or you can pad up and play against Wayne Gretzky and Mark Messier, who fire sponge pucks at full speed from a video screen.

A hockey tour From the entrance lobby, you pass into the NHL Zone, with multimedia displays and memorabilia about all aspects of the NHL and its milestone moments and teams. From there it's an exciting journey through the world of hockey, including an interactive Broadcast Zone, simulators, theaters showing hockey events, displays of artifacts and trophies, a re-creation of the Montréal Canadiens locker room, places to pick up some memorabilia of your own, and more. Before you leave check out the fun Our Game bronze and Team Canada '72 monument outside the building.

The lofty 19th-century building that houses this market is entirely worthy of the rich and colorful displays within. This is the place to taste a Canadian peameal bacon sandwich or buy the ingredients for a picnic banquet.

Food-lovers' favorites There are more than 50 vendors in the market, all of them experts in their own specialty, and the array of cheeses, meats, vegetables, deli goods, seafood, baked goods and gourmet treats is irresistible. At Sausage King you'll find 10 or more types of salami. Combine any one with the breads at the Carousel Bakery or grab a peameal bacon sandwich for breakfast (the flavor of the bacon is deliciously enriched by its coating of ground dried peas). Go to Carnicero's for local beef, pulled pork burritos and meat pies. Great wheels of cheese can be found at Alex Farm Products—from Stilton to Camembert. Any picnic will be enhanced by the chocolate butter tarts, skor brownies or other pastries sold at Future Bakery. And for good measure, why not throw in some Quebec terrines (rabbit and pistachio, wild boar and apricot, pheasant and mushroom), pâtés, or shrimp and lobster mousse from Scheffler's Deli? Downstairs there's more, including Caviar Direct and 33 different kinds of rice at Rube's.

Fresh from the fields On Saturday farmers set up stalls at daybreak in the Farmers' Market building across the street, selling fresh produce, preserves, fresh baking, meat, and arts and crafts.

THE BASICS

www.stlawrencemarket.com
+ N7
✉ 92 Front Street East
☎ 416/392-7219
🕐 Tue–Thu 8–6, Fri 8–7, Sat 5–5; farmers' market Sat 5am–3pm
🚇 King or Union
🚌 504 King streetcar
♿ Good
♨ Free

HIGHLIGHTS

● Sausage King
● Carousel Bakery
● Carnicero's
● Future Bakery
● Scheffler's Deli
● Alex Farm Products
● Caviar Direct

More to See

ALLAN GARDENS

Just a short way east of busy Yonge Street, this peaceful haven is a horticultural gem. It has six greenhouses, of which the best is the glass-domed Palm House, modeled on the one at Kew Gardens in London, which stands here in radiant Victorian glory.

➕ N4 ✉ 19 Horticultural Avenue, off Gerrard Street ☎ 416/392-7288 🕐 Daily 10–5 🚇 College ♿ Good 🎟 Free

MACKENZIE HOUSE

Toronto's first mayor, William Lyon Mackenzie, lived here from 1859 until his death in 1861 and it now acts as a museum recalling his life. As an outspoken journalist, he published the *Colonial Advocate*, and the house has a re-creation of his printshop. Other displays recall his turbulent political life, including the unsuccessful Upper Canada Rebellion that he led.

➕ M5 ✉ 82 Bond Street ☎ 416/392-6915 🕐 May–early Sep Tue–Sun 12–5; Sep–Dec Tue–Fri 12–4, Sat–Sun 12–5; Jan–Apr Sat–Sun 12–5 🚇 Dundas ♿ Few 🎟 Inexpensive

OSGOODE HALL

www.osgoodehall.com

This building (1829) houses the headquarters of Ontario's legal profession, with an elegant interior and an impressive portrait and sculpture collection. There are many rooms to see, including the stunning Great Library and American Room, the courtrooms, and Convocation Hall, with its superb stained-glass windows. Throughout, there are outstanding tiled floors and other architectural features. The building is set in grounds of lawns and flower beds. While there, try the Osgoode Hall Restaurant for lunch (▷ 57–58)

➕ L6 ✉ 130 Queen Street West ☎ 416/947-3300 🕐 Mon–Fri 8.30–5 🚇 Osgoode ♿ Few 🎟 Free

TEXTILE MUSEUM OF CANADA

www.textilemuseum.ca

This gem of a museum has a huge permanent collection of 12,000 textiles, some as old as 2,000 years, from all over the world. There are also changing exhibitions offering collections that are esthetically

A splendid hat on display (above) and a silk kimono (right) at the Textile Museum of Canada

engaging as well as of anthropological interest.

🔲 L5 ⊠ 55 Centre Avenue ☎ 416/599-5321 🕐 Daily 11–5 (Wed to 8) 🚇 St. Patrick ♿ Very good 💵 Moderate

TORONTO EATON CENTRE

www.torontoeatoncentre.com

Timothy Eaton emigrated from Ireland in 1865 and set up shop in St. Mary's, Ontario. He arrived in Toronto in 1869 and opened a store on Yonge Street, where he started innovative merchandizing and marketing, like fixed prices, cash-only sales, refunds and mail order—all unique then. Sadly, Eaton's was eventually swallowed up in the Sears Canada group. Enter at the southern end to see the splendor of Ed Zeidler's 264m (866ft) galleria and the sculptured flock of 60 Canada geese in flight by Michael Snow.

🔲 M5 ⊠ Dundas and Yonge to Queen and Yonge ☎ 416/598-8760 🕐 Mon–Fri 10–9, Sat 9.30–9.30, Sun 10–7 🍴 Several restaurants plus food court 🚇 Dundas or Queen ♿ Very good 💵 Free

TORONTO SCULPTURE GARDEN

www.torontosculpturegarden.com

A serene retreat established in 1981 in a city park. Two installations annually feature works by Canadian and international artists. The space offers artists the chance to experiment in a public context. The works are for sale.

🔲 N7 ⊠ 115 King Street East at Church ☎ 416/515-9658 🕐 Daily 8–dusk 🚇 King 💵 Free

TRINITY SQUARE AND TORONTO PUBLIC LABYRINTH

When plans for the Toronto Eaton Centre were drawn up, they called for the demolition of the Church of the Holy Trinity. Fortunately it was saved, and now sits in a little park just west of the Toronto Eaton Centre. Built in 1847, the church now overlooks a labyrinth, some 23m (77ft) across, installed in 2005. The theory is that by walking in these ever-decreasing circles you will center yourself and thus aid creative thinking or gain a problem-solving mind-set. It's worth a try.

🔲 M5 🚇 Dundas

The colorful Allan Gardens

Toronto Eaton Centre and the sculptured geese by Michael Snow

Historic Highlights

Explore some of Toronto's oldest areas, including the Distillery Historic District and one of the best food markets in Canada.

DISTANCE: 3km (2 miles) **ALLOW:** 3 hours

START ....

UNION STATION
✚ L7 🚇 Union Square

END ....

TORONTO SCULPTURE PARK
✚ N7 🚇 King

❶ From Union Station, walk east on Front Street, cross over Yonge Street to pass the Sony Centre and St. Lawrence Centre for the Arts.

❷ Check out the mural on the wall of the Flatiron Building, then cross Church Street and continue to St. Lawrence Market.

❸ After exploring the market, turn right down Jarvis Street, then go left to walk along The Esplanade alongside David Crombie Park.

❹ At the end, go forward into Parliament Square park (a plaque relates to the site of the first parliament buildings), then cross Parliament Street and walk along Mill Street. Turn right to explore the Distillery Historic District.

❽ Reach Jarvis Street, cross diagonally and enter St. James Park to see the Cathedral Church of St. James (1844), once the city's tallest building. Opposite, across King Street, is Toronto Sculpture Garden.

❼ Turn right here, and go up Frederick Street into the Old Town Heritage Area, site of the original settlement. At the end of Frederick Street turn left on Adelaide, passing Toronto's First Post Office.

❻ Continue west across several intersections, passing the Imperial Oil Opera Theatre (note the mural on the Toronto Sun building opposite) and the Young People's Theatre.

❺ Exit the Distillery site onto Mill Street, cross and walk north on Trinity Street. Turn left onto Front Street, with distant views of the downtown skyscrapers.

Shopping

BAY OF SPIRITS GALLERY

www.bayofspirits.com
Sells a wide range of First Nations artwork including Ojibway, Iroquois, Inuit, and Haida art.
🔶 L7 ⊠ 156 Front Street West ☎ 416/971-5190 Ⓜ Union

BEN MCNALLY BOOKS

www.benmcnallybooks.com
This excellent independent bookseller has a loyal following and a warm, wood-paneled space that's reminiscent of an old library.
🔶 L6 ⊠ 366 Bay Street ☎ 416/361-0032 🚋 501 Queen streetcar

BROOKFIELD PLACE

www.brookfieldplacenewsandevents.com
Formerly known as BCE Place, this is worth a visit just to walk through the stunning Allen Lambert Galleria. It's home to about 50 stores and services (and the Hockey Hall of Fame), and links to Union Station, the Air Canada Centre and the PATH system.
🔶 M7 ⊠ 181 Bay Street ☎ 416/777-6480 Ⓜ Union

BULLOCH TAILORS

www.bullochtailors.com
This is where the city's professional, political and military men come to be kitted out. Bespoke suits begin at $995.
🔶 M7 ⊠ 43 Colborne Street ☎ 416/367-1084 Ⓜ King

COLLEGE PARK & ATRIUM ON BAY

www.atriumtoronto.com
The first is an Art Deco landmark with five stores; the second is an '80s building, with 60 stores.
🔶 M4 Ⓜ College 🔶 M5 Ⓜ Dundas

CORKTOWN DESIGNS

www.corktowndesigns.com
Unique items of jewelry from more than 50 contemporary Canadian and international artists.
🔶 Q7 ⊠ Building 54, 55 Mill Street ☎ 416/861-3020 🚋 504 King streetcar

DANIEL ET DANIEL

www.danieletdaniel.ca
All kinds of foods—from a croissant for breakfast to pâtés, pizzas, salads and hors d'oeuvres for lunch.
🔶 P4 ⊠ 248 Carlton Street ☎ 416/968-9275 🚋 506 Carlton streetcar

FIRST CANADIAN PLACE

www.myfirstcanadianplace.ca
At the base of this towering office complex, a gleaming three-level mall has around 120 stores.
🔶 L6–L7 ⊠ 100 King Street ☎ 416/862-3138 Ⓜ King

HAVEN

www.havenshop.ca
Loft-like men's clothing store in Corktown. While the T-shirts are on the pricey side, the sneakers and backpacks here are unique and worthwhile.
🔶 P6 ⊠ 145 Berkeley Street ☎ 647/344-4745 🚋 501 Queen streetcar

HUDSON'S BAY

www.thebay.com
Designer boutiques and a pleasant store to shop in.
🔶 M6 ⊠ 176 Yonge at Queen ☎ 416/861-9111 Ⓜ Queen

TORONTO EATON CENTRE

www.torontoeatoncentre.com
A million visitors a week shop in this indoor mall on four levels (▷ 53).
🔶 M5–M6 ⊠ Yonge between Dundas and Queen ☎ 416/598-8560 Ⓜ Dundas or Queen

Entertainment and Nightlife

AIR CANADA CENTRE
www.theaircanadacentre.com
Principally the home of the Toronto Maple Leafs hockey team, this stadium also stages superstar concerts.
➕ L8 ✉ 40 Bay Street
☎ 416/815-5500 🚇 Union

BERKELEY STREET THEATRE
www.canadianstage.com
In a converted historic building, this is one of the theaters of the Canadian Stage Company.
➕ P7 ✉ 26 Berkeley Street
☎ 416/367-8243 🚋 504 King Streetcar

C'EST WHAT
www.cestwhat.com
A comfortable cellar-style bar for quiet conversation and folk-acoustic music.
➕ M7 ✉ 67 Front Street East ☎ 416/867-9499
🚇 Union

ED MIRVISH THEATRE
www.mirvish.com
This 1920s theatre stages high-profile productions, and was once home to the largest cinema in Canada with 3,373 seats.
➕ M5 ✉ 244 Victoria Street
☎ 416/872-1212 TicketKing
🚇 Dundas or Queen

ELGIN AND WINTER GARDEN THEATRES
www.heritagetrust.on.ca
A National Historic Site owned by the Ontario Heritage Trust, this is the only double-decker theater still in existence. It is worth a visit just to see the restoration. If you can't get tickets, take a guided tour.
➕ M6 ✉ 189 Yonge Street
☎ 416/314-2901 🚇 Queen

FOUR SEASONS CENTRE FOR THE PERFORMING ARTS
www.coc.ca
Opened in 2006 as the home of the Canadian Opera Company and the National Ballet of Canada, this magnificent theater has the latest technological and acoustic features.
➕ L6 ✉ 145 Queen Street West ☎ 416/363-6671
🚇 Osgoode

MASSEY HALL
www.masseyhall.com
One of the most popular live music venues in the city.

DISTILLERY ARTS
The Distillery Historic District is a cultural center housing professional theater and dance companies, including the acclaimed Soulpepper Theatre Company, Native Earth Performing Arts, Tapestry New Opera Works, DanceWork, Volcano, Tapestry New Opera Works and the Nightwood Theatre. The complex also includes a theater museum, a performing arts college and the superb **Young Centre for the Performing Arts** (✉ Buildings 50 ☎ 416/866-8666).

➕ M6 ✉ 178 Victoria Street
☎ 416/872-4255 🚇 Queen

NOW LOUNGE
www.nowtoronto.com
An interesting program of Canadian and international acts is presented in this intimate little place in the *NOW Magazine* building.
➕ M6 ✉ 189 Church Street
☎ 416/532-7020 🚇 Queen or Dundas

THE RESERVOIR LOUNGE
www.reservoirlounge.com
Cool, lower-level spot, with proper martinis and nightly live jazz. Decent food menu too with an Asian flair.
➕ M7 ✉ 52 Wellington Street East ☎ 416/955-0887
🚋 504 King streetcar

ST. LAWRENCE CENTRE FOR THE ARTS
www.stlc.com
Dedicated to providing a diverse program of high-quality cultural events.
➕ M7 ✉ 27 Front Street East ☎ 416/366-7723,
1-800/708-6754 box office, 416/366-1656 (admin)
🚇 Union

SONY CENTRE FOR THE PERFORMING ARTS
www.sonycentre.ca
This important venue hosts special big-name concerts, multimedia presentations and short-run shows.
➕ M7 ✉ 1 Front Street East
☎ 1-855/872-7669 🚇 Union

Restuarants

PRICES

Prices are approximate, based on a 3-course meal for one person.

$$$$	over $80
$$$	$60–$80
$$	$35–$60
$	under $35

BB33 ($$)

www.bb33.ca

The bistro is the more formal choice for dinner, with dishes such as braised venison, osso buco or duck with cinnamon and raisin couscous. The brasserie has great buffets and a good à la carte menu.

⊞ L4 ⊠ 33 Gerrard Street West ☎ 416/585-4319 ⓒ Bistro: Mon–Sat 5–10pm; Brasserie: Mon–Sat 7–11am, 12–2, 5–9.30, Sun 12–2 (brunch) Ⓠ Dundas or College

BYMARK ($$$$)

www.bymark.ca

Dramatic decor of wood, glass and water with a delectable menu of classics and service to match. A bar one floor up offers extreme comfort and views. Summer patio.

⊞ L7 ⊠ 66 Wellington Street West ☎ 416/777-1144 ⓒ Lunch Mon–Fri; dinner Mon–Sat Ⓠ Union

CANOE ($$$$)

www.canoerestaurant.com

On the 54th floor of the TDC Bank Tower. Inventive cuisine makes use of Canadian ingredients (West Coast halibut, Alberta lamb, Grandview venison).

⊞ L7 ⊠ 66 Wellington Street West ☎ 416/364-0054 ⓒ Lunch and dinner Mon–Fri Ⓠ Union

ESPLANADE BIER MARKT ($$)

www.thebiermarkt.com

A traditional Belgian-themed tile, wood and brick bistro where mussels and french fries are king. More than 100 bottled beers and more are available on tap.

⊞ P7 ⊠ 58 The Esplanade ☎ 416/862-7575 ⓒ Sun–Wed 11am–1am, Thu–Sat 11am–2am Ⓠ Union

FRAN'S ($)

www.fransrestaurant.com

A massive menu and 24-hour opening make for a real downtown

ONTARIO WINES

Since the VQA (Vintners' Quality Alliance) appellation was introduced in 1988, Ontario's wines have improved immensely, and now you will find them on the very best wine lists. Look for Cave Spring, Konzelmann, Stoney Ridge and the big names—Inniskillin, Château des Charmes and Trius Winery at Hillebrand. Canada's ice wine is internationally known. Made from grapes that have frozen on the vine, it is thick, rich and sweet—delicious with *biscotti.*

pleaser. There are a dozen or more breakfast choices, plus soups, salads, sandwiches, burgers, steak, ribs, chicken, seafood, pasta, fajitas and classic comfort food.

⊞ M5 ⊠ 200 Victoria Street ☎ 416/304-0085 ⓒ 24 hours Ⓠ Queen or Dundas

IRISH EMBASSY PUB & GRILL ($$)

www.irishembassypub.com

Upscale to suit the splendid old bank building it occupies, this place is renowned for its food, from hot breakfasts, through lunchtime sandwiches and bar snacks to entrées, including Irish stew and Kilkenny battered haddock with fries.

⊞ M7 ⊠ 49 Yonge Street ☎ 416/866-8282 ⓒ Mon–Fri 11.30am–2am, Sat–Sun 11am–2am Ⓠ King

NAMI ($$)

www.namirestaurant.ca

Ultrastylish and very expensive, this restaurant is frequented by Japanese business people and their guests. Prime attractions are the really fresh sushi and sashimi and darkly sophisticated interior.

⊞ M6 ⊠ 55 Adelaide Street East ☎ 416/362-7373 ⓒ Lunch Mon–Fri; dinner Mon–Sat Ⓠ Queen or King

OSGOODE HALL RESTAURANT ($)

www.lsuc.on.ca

Inside the Court of Appeal for Ontario historic

building you'll find this fine French lunch spot filled with judges and old law books. The food and the service are both excellent; and the prix-fixe three-course menu is very fairly priced.

⊞ L6 ⊠ 130 Queen Street West ☎ 416/47-3361 ⓒ Lunch Mon–Fri. Closed Jul–Aug 🚋 501 Queen streetcar

RICHTREE NATURAL MARKET ($)

www.richtreenaturalmarket.com
This vast indoor European market, with the world's foods made fresh to order at the cooking stations, is excellent value for money . There's an in-house bakery, too. Fill up your tray and choose a table in any one of seven themed areas.

⊞ M4 ⊠ 444 Yonge Street ☎ 416/849-9241 ⓒ Mon–Fri 6.30am–6.30pm, Sat 8am–5pm 🚇 Union 🚋 506 Carlton streetcar

RUTH'S CHRIS STEAK HOUSE ($$$)

www.ruthschris.ca
Early dinners and its proximity to a number of theaters and other entertainment venues make this an ideal choice for pre-show meals. In addition to the steaks, there are seafood, chicken and a range of other choices.

⊞ L6 ⊠ 145 Richmond Street West ☎ 416/955-1455 or 1-800/544-0808 ⓒ Dinner daily, lunch Fri 🚇 Osgoode

SENATOR ($–$$)

www.thesenator.com
Claiming to be the city's oldest restaurant, the Senator is in a fine old building and offers good-value comfort food, such as homemade meat loaf with mashed potatoes, liver and onions, and fish-and-chips.

⊞ M5 ⊠ 249 Victoria Street ☎ 416/364-7517 ⓒ Breakfast and lunch daily, dinner Tue–Sat 🚇 Dundas

STARFISH ($$)

www.starfishoysterbed.com
The owner of this comfy

TORONTO EATON CENTRE

Shopping mall eating conjures up fluorescent-lit food courts, meals in a bag and paper cups of coffee, but in the Toronto Eaton Centre you can do much better. Try **Baton Rouge**, famous for its succulent ribs, with intimate booths and tables and subdued lighting (⊠ Street level ☎ 416/593-9667); the **City Kitchen**, a casual family-friendly restaurant with hearty Canadian comfort foods such as poutine, salmon burgers and pulled pork sandwiches (⊠ Street level ☎ 416/519-5839). Before you rule out the food court, note it contains **The Urban Eatery**, part of a $120 million revitalization project and offers some excellent express eats.

---

and friendly restaurant is a walking encyclopedia of seafood lore. The tempting array of oysters, oven-roasted black cod and east coast lobsters is just too good to resist.

⊞ N6 ⊠ 100 Adelaide Street East ☎ 416/366-7827 ⓒ Lunch Mon–Fri; dinner daily 🚇 King

THE SULTAN'S TENT & CAFÉ MOROC ($$)

www.thesultanstent.com
With a sumptuously tented interior, this fine restaurant offers delicious and beautifully presented Moroccan food, including tender tagines and flavoursome couscous dishes. The fixed-price four-course meals are excellent value, the service is good and the nightly belly-dancing shows are a bonus.

⊞ M7 ⊠ 49 Front Street East ☎ 416/961-0601 ⓒ Lunch and dinner Mon–Sat, Sun dinner 🚇 Union

TUNDRA ($$$)

Well-named for its focus on Canadian cuisine and wines, even the decor evokes the barren north. The dinner menu might include such dishes as grilled B.C. octopus and smoked Haida Gwaii black cod or Dufferin county lamb loin.

⊞ L6 ⊠ Hilton Hotel, 145 Richmond Street West ☎ 416/860-6800 ⓒ Breakfast, lunch and dinner daily 🚇 Osgoode

This is where Toronto relaxes—the south-facing strip alongside Lake Ontario. There are parks, traffic-free paths for walking, cycling and rollerblading, open-air stages and restaurants. The water is busy with kayaks, sailboats and ferries to the islands.

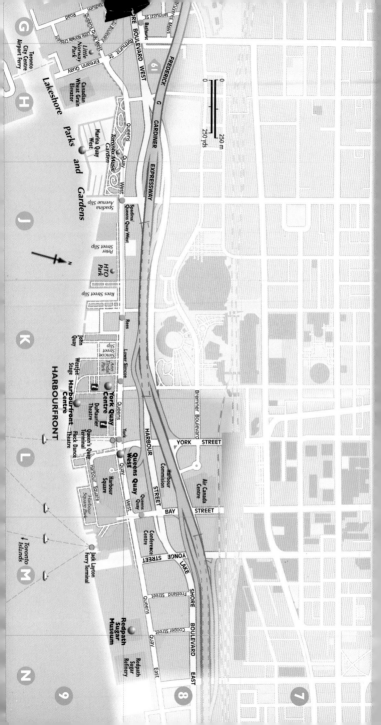

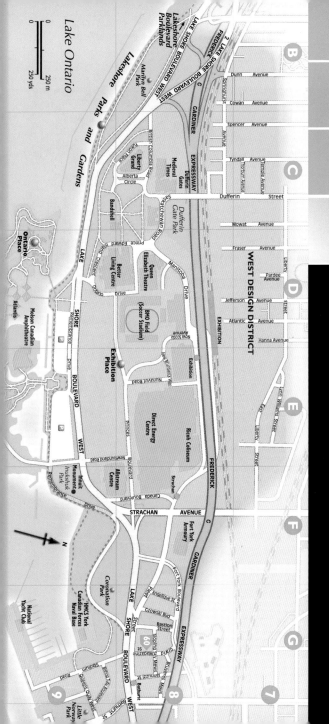

Lake Ontario

0 — 250 m
0 — 250 yds

N

Lakeshore Parks and Gardens

Lakeshore Boulevard Parklands

LAKE SHORE BOULEVARD WEST
FREDERICK BOULEVARD

GARDINER EXPRESSWAY

2 LAKE SHORE BOULEVARD

Dunn Avenue
Springhurst
Cowan Avenue
Spencer Avenue
Avenue
Tyndall Avenue
Temple Avenue
Thorburn Avenue
Dufferin Street
Mowat Avenue
Fraser Avenue
Liberty Street
Pardee Avenue
Jefferson Avenue
Atlantic Avenue
Hanna Avenue

WEST DESIGN DISTRICT

Marilyn Bell Park

British Columbia Road
Yukon Place
Liberty Grand
Alberta Circle
Medieval Times
Dufferin Gates
Dufferin Gate Park

Bandshell

Saskatchewan Road
Manitoba Drive
Prince Edward Island Crescent
Ontario Drive

Better Living Centre

Queen Elizabeth Theatre
BMO Field (Soccer Stadium)
Exhibition Place

New Scotia Avenue
New Brunswick Way
Nunavut Road
Exhibition

EXHIBITION

LAKE SHORE BOULEVARD WEST

Ontario Place
Atlantis
Molson Canadian Amphitheatre

Remembrance Drive

Direct Energy Centre
Ricoh Coliseum
Allstream Centre

Princes Boulevard
Canada Boulevard
Newfoundland Road

Inukshuk Monument
Inukshuk Park
Remembrance Drive

STRACHAN AVENUE
Strachan
FREDERICK

Fort York Armoury

GARDINER EXPRESSWAY

Coronation Park
HMCS York Canadian Forces Naval Base

National Yacht Club

Fort York Boulevard
Fleet Street
Angelique St
Czowski Blvd
Bastion Street
Stadium Road

LAKE SHORE BOULEVARD WEST

Shoring St Marks
Magazine St
Grand Magazine St
Janual St
Bruyère St Marks

Little Norway Park
Bathurst St

Dunn Williams Street
Liberty Street
Liberty Street
East Liberty Street

9 8 7
B C D E F G

Harbourfront Centre

TOP 25

HIGHLIGHTS

● Shopping at Queen's Quay
● Art exhibits at The Power Plant and Bill Boyle Artport
● Craft Studio
● Performances
● Free weekend festivals
● Lake View Market

TIPS

● Winter is just as much fun at Harbourfront with its large outdoor skating rink.
● Harbourfront Centre is on the Waterfront Trail.

This development is a wonderful example of a waterfront park that is not simply a glorified shopping mall. It's a place to spend the whole day—biking, sailing, canoeing, picnicking, watching crafts-people—and even shopping.

Lakefront leisure Start at Queen's Quay Terminal (▷ 69) where there is an attractive shopping mall with specialty shops housed in an old warehouse building. Several restaurants have outside dining areas from which to enjoy the waterfront. Take the lakeside walking trail to Bill Boyle Artport, stopping en route at the Power Plant, a contemporary art gallery, and The Harbourfront Centre behind it. At Bill Boyle Artport you'll find artisans glass-making, pot-throwing, jewelry-making, silk-screening or metal-sculpting. You can purchase the results in

Clockwise from left: Queen's Quay Terminal interior and exterior; the Du Maurier Theatre; Bill Boyle Artport, exterior and interior views

the adjacent store. York Quay's lakefront has a small pond, a children's play area and the outdoor WestJet Stage. Across the footbridge is John Quay, which has several restaurants.

The place to rent a boat In good weather, Harbourfront is a great place to relax on the grass or people-watch from one of the waterfront cafés. Alternatively, sail- and powerboats can be rented or you can sign up for sailing lessons at Habourfront Centre Sailing and Powerboating (tel 416/203-3000).

Festivals and events Harbourfront holds more than 4,000 events of all sorts, from the Milk International Children's Festival of the Arts to the International Festival of Authors in October and the LunarFest in January.

THE BASICS

www.harbourfrontcentre.com
🔌 L9
✉ Harbourfront Centre, 235 Queens Quay West
☎ 416/973-4000
🕐 Bill Boyle Artport daily 10am–11pm (to 9pm Sun). Queen's Quay daily from 10am
🍴 Several
🚋 510 Spadina streetcar from Union
♿ Very good
💲 Free
❓ Many special events (information at Bill Boyle Artport)

HIGHLIGHTS

- Sandy beaches
- Centre Island
- Hanlan's Point
- View from Algonquin Island

TIPS

- If you're planning a picnic, don't bring alcohol—you need to order it in advance and pick it up from Centreville Catering (☎ 416/203-0405).
- Barbecue pits are available, but it's best to bring a portable charcoal barbecue in case they are all taken.

A mere 15-minute ferry ride takes you to this peaceful archipelago with meandering waterways, cycle paths and bucolic lanes, which seems light years away from the bustling city you left behind.

A city retreat Originally a peninsula, inundated by the sea in a storm in 1858, the 14 Toronto Islands incorporate 243ha (600 acres) laced with waterways and inlets. People come to walk, cycle, play tennis, feed the ducks, picnic, sit on the beach or go boating. There are swimming areas on Centre and Ward's Island (and a "clothing optional" beach at Hanlan's Point) but they are often polluted.

The main areas These are Centre Island, Ward's Island and Hanlan's Point. The first is the busiest, with Centreville—an old-fashioned amusement

Clockwise from left: Centreville amusement on Centre Island; Toronto's marina and the small Hanlan's Point; a ferry arriving at the Toronto Island docks; Canada geese on the islands; Hanlan's Point

park with an 1890s carousel, a flume ride and antique cars—and a small working farm where children can pet the lambs and ride the ponies. From Centre Island a bridge crosses over the main watercourse (with boats for rent) to the arc of the former peninsula, with Ward's Island to the east and Hanlan's Point to the west. There are sandy beaches all the way round the outer edge and a central pier juts out into the lake. Behind the beaches pathways crisscross lawns dotted with trees, and there are barbecue pits, picnic tables and a kids' playground. Another big attraction for children is the delightful Franklin Children's Garden. Ward's Island is the main residential spot, while the western area includes the Gibraltar Point Lighthouse, Artscape Gibraltar Point and—closest to the mainland—the City Airport. To explore, rent a bike or take the Island Tram Tour.

THE BASICS

➕ Off map south of harbor. Ferries M9
☎ Centreville 416/203-0405. Ferry 416/392-8193
🍴 Several options
🚋 509 Harbourfront streetcar or Bay 6 and Spadina 77B buses to Ferry Docks
🚢 Approximately every 15 minutes in summer but less frequently in winter
♿ Few
💰 Ferry moderate
❓ Seasonal events

More to See

EXHIBITION PLACE

www.explace.on.ca

Housing the Direct Energy Centre, BMO Field (the 21,500-seat national soccer stadium), RICOH Coliseum (home of the Toronto Marlies hockey team), Canada's Sport Hall of Fame, the Horse Palace riding academy and Toronto's renewable energy cooperative, there's plenty going on year-round, but the highlight is the annual Canadian National Exhibition. It's one of the largest events of its kind in North America and includes exhibitors, attractions, midway rides, dog and horse shows, performances, an air show, shopping and food stands. ✚ E8 ✉ Off Lake Shore Boulevard, Strachan Avenue and Dufferin Street ☎ 416/263-3330 (Canadian National Exhibition only) 🚋 509 Harbourfront, 511 Bathurst streetcars 🚇 Exhibition

LAKESHORE PARKS AND GARDENS

www.toronto.ca/parks

The lakeshore is the resort area of the city. Between the malls, entertainment venues, hotels and marinas a number of green spaces have also been created. They are all on the Martin Goodman Trail, the Toronto section of the Waterfront Trail, which stretches for 1,400km (870 miles) along Lake Ontario and beyond. One of the newer parks is HTO Park, which opened in 2007 and was instantly popular, not least for its sandy beach dotted with umbrellas.

A short walk to the west is the 0.8ha (2-acre) Toronto Music Garden, where the design concept, a collaboration between landscaper Julie Moir Messervy and cellist Yo Yo Ma, was to represent Bach's First Suite for Unaccompanied Cello. Areas convey the movements of the piece and free concerts are staged here in summer.

Next is Little Norway Park, a small area west of the grain elevator that gives access to the ferry for the City Airport on the Islands. Turn right at the end of Queen's Quay West and the trail goes off-road into the wide expanse of Coronation Park. There's a naval base in one corner and National

The Canadian National Exhibition

Queens Quay West

Yacht Club and Alexandra Yacht Club facilities jut into the lake. The park has picnic areas and three softball pitches. There is also the World War II 50th Anniversary Memorial and some commemorative tree plantings. At the western end is the Inukshuk monument, an Inuit symbol in the shape of a stone man.

From here the trail continues between Ontario Place and Exhibition Place to Marilyn Bell Park, which blends into the Lakeshore Boulevard Parklands, where locals come to walk their dogs or play tennis.

✚ C9 ☎ 416/392-1111 🚌 509 Harbourfront, 510 Spadina streetcars

ONTARIO PLACE

www.ontarioplace.com

Built in the 1970s, the futuristic-looking Ontario Place used to be home to a large waterpark. It was closed in 2012, as the entire area is currently being redeveloped with a targeted completion date of 2017, just in time for Canada's 150th anniversary. The Ontario government will spend up to $100 million on transforming Ontario Place into a year-round waterfront destination.

One of the first new developments has been the Urban Park & Waterfront Trail project., situated right on Toronto's prime waterfront. The Waterfront Trail is an existing series of trails that run 1,400km (875 miles) along the shores of Lake Ontario and beyond.

Further plans include more green space, a museum, a canal district lined with stores and restaurants, and a year-round music and festival venue. Concerts at the Molson Canadian Amphitheatre and Echo Beach will continue during the construction, and the marina and Atlantis pavilions will remain open. The IMAX movie theater inside the geodesic Cinesphere is closed but this unique building will be conserved as an important part of the site's cultural heritage. The same goes for the Eberhard Zeidler-designed steel and glass pods.

✚ D9 ✉ 955 Lake Shore Boulevard West ☎ 416/341-9900 🕐 Mon–Fri 10–12, 1–3.30 ✋ Free 🚇 Union 🚌 509 Harbourfront or 511 Bathurst streetcars, then walk south ♿ Good

QUEENS QUAY WEST

Stretching from the bottom of Bay Street west to the foot of Bathurst, Queens Quay West has become one of the city's hotspots. In addition to giving access to attractions such as the Harbourfront Centre (▷62–63) and several waterfront parks, it is lined by restaurants, hotels, and good specialty stores and malls. A number of high-rise condo buildings here form some of the hottest real estate in the city.

✚ L9

REDPATH SUGAR MUSEUM

www.redpathsugars.com

If you have a half-hour or so to spare, this unusual little museum tells the story of the company that has refined and sold sugar and sugar products in Canada since 1853. It has displays about sugarcane, sugar beet, refining methods, the slave trade and social aspects of sugar.

✚ M8 ✉ 95 Queens Quay East ☎ 416/366-3561 🕐 Mon–Fri 10–12, 1–3.30 ✋ Free 🚇 Union Station 🚌 6 ♿ Good

An Island Stroll

Take a ferry ride to discover an offshore haven, with parkland and beaches, bikes and boating, and spectacular views of the city.

DISTANCE: 2.5km (1.5 miles) **ALLOW:** 3 hours

START

TORONTO ISLANDS PIER
➕ M9 🚌 Pier area

END

TORONTO ISLANDS PIER
➕ M9 🚌 Pier area

❶ From the Toronto Islands Ferry Terminal take the ferry to Centre Island. Cross the square to the island information booth in the far left corner then go left on the path that leads past Centreville to the bridge.

❽ As an alternative, from Ward's Island Beach you can turn right onto the boardwalk, which will take you back to the pier area.

❷ Cross the bridge and continue past the fountain, through the gardens to the beach and pier for a look southward over the lake.

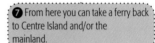

❼ From here you can take a ferry back to Centre Island and/or the mainland.

❸ Retrace your steps to the fountain, then turn right and follow the path to the boathouse. Loop around the back of the boathouse and continue to the pretty little church of St. Andrews by the Lake.

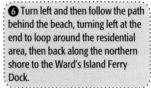

❻ Turn left and then follow the path behind the beach, turning left at the end to loop around the residential area, then back along the northern shore to the Ward's Island Ferry Dock.

❹ Continue on the same path, with occasional spectacular views across the water to the downtown sky-scrapers. Later pass the bridge (on your left) to Algonquin Island.

❺ Walk past the Island Canoe Club building, then turn right to Ward's Island Beach.

Shopping

THE CENTRE SHOP

www.harbourfrontcentre.com
Within the Bill Boyle Artport, part of the Harbourfront Centre, this is a terrific crafts shop showcasing contemporary Canadian works. These include pieces made by the center's resident artists, who can often be seen at work in the studios here.

L9 ⊠ 235 Queens Quay West ☎ 416/973-4993 ⊙ Daily 11–6 (to 8pm Thu and Fri) ⊕ Union

KITCHEN TABLE

www.the kitchentable.ca
If you are looking for picnic supplies to take to the islands or one of the lakeshore parks, look no farther than this store with bakery and deli goods and fresh fruit.

L8 ⊠ 10 Queens Quay West ☎ 416/777-9874 ⊙ Daily 6am–midnight ⊕ Union

LAKE VIEW MARKET

www.harbourfrontcentre.com
Stands selling crafts, jewelry, textiles and other goods from all over the world are set up on one of the quays at the Harbourfront Centre every summer weekend.

L9 ☎ 416/973-4000 ⊕ Union

LCBO

The Liquor Control Board of Ontario store has a great selection of wines, including Canadian varieties, beers that are kept in

a cold room, spirits and the fixings for cocktails.

M8 ⊠ 2 Cooper Street, Queen's Quay ☎ 416/864-6863 ⊙ Mon–Sat 9am–10pm, Sun 12–6 ⊕ Union

QUEEN'S QUAY TERMINAL

www.qqterminal.com
This upscale mall is a glittering space right on the lakeshore with an interesting selection of stores, including fashions, homewares, crafts, perfumes, toys, jewelry. Standouts include the Canadian Naturalist store, stocked full with quality Canadian-made clothing, crafts, and specialty foods, and the Museum of Inuit Art, with crafts for sale. There are several

THE TILLEY STORY

All Alex Tilley wanted was a good quality cotton hat to wear on fishing trips. It turned out that he had to invent one. It found such favor that over the last couple of decades the business has grown into an international success. In addition to the six stores in Toronto, Montréal, Mississauga and Vancouver, Tilley supplies retailers throughout Canada, the US, Chile, Europe, Australasia, Japan, Singapore, Bermuda, and the Turks and Caicos Islands. The range now includes all kinds of outdoor and travel clothing and accessories. For more information, see www.tilley.com.

excellent restaurants with lakefront patios.

L9 ⊠ 207 Queens Quay West ☎ 416/203-0510 ⊙ Wed–Sat 10–9, Sun–Tue 10–6 (hours may change seasonally) ⊕ Union 510 Spadina streetcar

TILLEY ENDURABLES

www.tilley.com
Bearing the name of the man who developed and designed the famous "Tilley Hat," which can be used for a variety of purposes in the wilderness, this store also stocks other great outdoors gear, including lightweight underwear, waterproofs and a multipocketed jacket that is invaluable for photographers. The flagship store is on Don Mills Road.

J9 ⊠ 207 Queens Quay West ☎ 416/203-0463 ⊕ Union ⊠ 900 Don Mills Road ☎ 647/351-3511

WHEEL EXCITEMENT

OK, it is not a store as such, but if you've watched the rollerbladers and cyclists zipping along the lakeshore routes and want to have a try, this is the place to rent the equipment. They rent in-line skates, mountain bikes and adult tricycles by the hour or the day, plus lessons. New and used equipment is sold off in the fall.

K9 ⊠ 249 Queens Quay West, Unit 106 ☎ 416/260-9000 ⊙ Mon–Wed 10–6, Thu–Sun 10–7 ⊕ Union

LAKESHORE AND ISLANDS SHOPPING

Entertainment and Nightlife

BMO FIELD

www.bmofield.com
Located at Exhibition Place, this soccer stadium has hosted two FIFA U-20 World Cups as well as international rugby games.

➕ D8 ✉ 170 Princes' Boulevard ☎ 416/360-4625 🚌 509 Harbourfront, 511 Bathurst streetcars 🚇 Exhibition

FIRKIN ON HARBOUR

www.firkinpubs.com
With 20 draft beers on tap and a waterfall-facing patio courtyard, this pub is perfect for a casual drink at the harbourfront. British-inspired decor and standard but good quality pub fare..

➕ M8 ✉ 10 Yonge Street ☎ 416/519-9949 🕐 Daily 11am–2am 🚇 Union

HARBOURFRONT CENTRE

www.harbourfrontcentre.com
This excellent not-for-profit entertainment and arts center (▷ 62–63) has events year-round, including concerts, dance, drama and festivals. It attracts performers and art forms that might not normally be seen in commercial venues, with a strong program of world music. The center's theaters include The Fleck Dance Theatre, which hosts a world-famous contemporary dance season and other events; the Harbourfront Centre Theatre puts on a variety of concerts, world music and dance; and the Studio Theatre has drama, kids' workshop productions and other events. There are also two open-air venues, the WestJet Stage, with an eclectic program of concerts, cabaret and comedy, and the Toronto Music Garden (▷ 66).

➕ K9–L9 ✉ 235 Queens Quay West ☎ 416/973-4000 box office, 416/973-4600 admin 🚇 Union

STREET MUSIC

When the weather is suitable, there's nothing Canadians like more than to be outside, and that applies to many of their musicians, too. There are plenty of organized open-air concerts, with the Harbourfront Centre, Dundas Square and the Distillery Historic District among popular venues, and you might even see one of the big-name local bands playing on a makeshift stage on a city square (particularly if they have a cause to support). Equally appealing (usually) are the street musicians you come across unexpectedly—anything from a guy with a guitar to a classical string quartet, and you won't use the subway for long before you hear one of the auditioned acts allowed to play down there.

MEDIEVAL TIMES DINNER & TOURNAMENT

www.medievaltimes.com
Jousting knights charge toward each other at high speed on Andalucian stallions while diners enjoy a multi-course feast preferred by serving wenches. The knights toss javelins and wield fierce-looking weapons, such as the bola and alabarda.

➕ C8 ✉ Exhibition Place, 10 Dufferin Street ☎ 416/260-1234 or 1-866/543-9637 🚌 509 Harbourfront, 511 Bathurst streetcars 🚇 Exhibition

POLSON PIER

www.polsonpier.com
Located on the water, Polson Pier offers all kinds of nightlife action for the young and young at heart. Head to the Sound Academy nightclub and you'll see what a million dollars in sight and sound feels and looks like. If you're looking for a party, then the Cabana Pool Bar transforms the waterfront into a day-to-night pool party. Solarium is a more intimate nightclub setting with a separate dance floor and a great Toronto skyline view. Other activities include karting, a golf driving range, volleyball, swimming pool, rock climbing range, drive-in and more.

➕ Q9 ✉ 11 Polson Street ☎ 416/469-5655 🚌 72A, 172

Restaurants

PRICES

Prices are approximate, based on a 3-course meal for one person.

$$$$	over $80
$$$	$60–$80
$$	$35–$60
$	under $35

ALEXANDROS TAKE-OUT ($)

This hole-in-the-wall is handily located by the waterfront of Westin Harbour Castle is great value and serves a great range of tasty Greek gyros, souvlakis and crispy fries with feta cheese. Eat at the nearby beach or on their little patio.

➕ M8 ✉ 5 Queens Quay West ☎ 416/367-0633 🕒 Daily 11 til late 🚋 509 Harbourfront streetcar

THE CAROUSEL CAFÉ ($)

On Centre Island, this lovely spot has great views of the city and it's a good place for a lazy lunch. There's plenty of outdoor seating with umbrellas for shade, and a menu of well-cooked dishes that will please the whole family.

➕ Off map ✉ Centreville, Centre Island ☎ 416/203-0405 🕒 Varies seasonally; call for details 🛳 Centre Island

HARBOUR SIXTY STEAKHOUSE ($$$)

www.harboursixty.com
Climb the stone steps to a gorgeous baroque-inspired foyer to enjoy some of the finest basic ingredients. Prime beef, tuna, lobsters on ice, Atlantic salmon and the best slow-roasted prime rib beef in town.

➕ L8 ✉ 60 Harbour Street ☎ 416/777-2111 🕒 Mon–Fri 11.30–5, Sat–Sun 5pm till late 🚇 Union

KOKORO SUSHI ($)

Daily specials are written on the blackboard at this simple sushi joint surrounded by condo highrises. Expect excellent value here for beautifully presented quality fish.

➕ M8 ✉ 16 Yonge Street ☎ 416/363-9379 🕒 Tue–Sun 11.30–10 🚇 Union

PICNIC PLACES

With all the fantastic parks lining the lakeshore, there's no shortage of perfect places to spread a blanket and lay out your feast. Many of the parks have picnic tables, too. Take the ferry over to the Toronto Islands and you will find not only tables, but also barbecue pits, though they get taken very quickly. If you take your own barbecue, only small, charcoal burning types are allowed on the ferry (they won't carry alcohol either). You can get supplies at the excellent Kitchen Table (▷ 69) or from the big Loblaws supermarket on Queens Quay East.

PEARL HARBOURFRONT RESTAURANT ($$)

www.pearlharbourfront.ca
As the name suggests, this restaurant offers a delightful lakefront dining experience, with authentic dishes—dim sum, Peking duck, braised lobster, noodle dishes, and much more is on the menu. Book a window seat here at the end of August and you will enjoy a great place from which watch the air show.

➕ L9 ✉ Queen's Quay Terminal, Main Level, 207 Queens Quay West ☎ 416/203-1233 🕒 Lunch and dinner daily 🚇 Union

RECTORY CAFÉ ($–$$)

www.therectorycafe.com
This delightful café is full of character, with the works of local artists on the walls and intimate seating. In good weather head to a table in the garden. The small menu features well-cooked dishes such as Prince Edward Islands (PEI) mussels or goat cheese salad, followed by salmon, vegetarian risotto and roasted chicken supreme. There is also an excellent range of lunchtime sandwiches that will appeal to all tastes and budgets.

➕ Off map ✉ 102 Lakeshore Avenue, Ward's Island ☎ 416/203-2152 🕒 Seasonal hours; call for details 🛳 Ward's Island

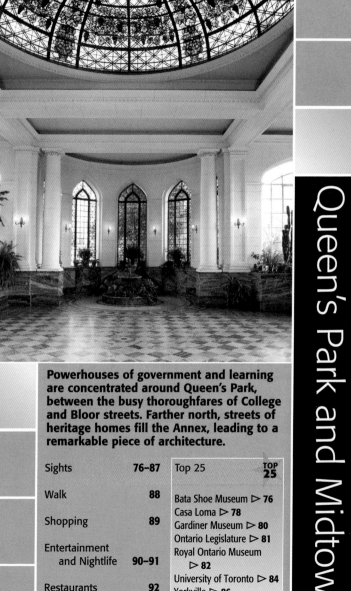

Powerhouses of government and learning are concentrated around Queen's Park, between the busy thoroughfares of College and Bloor streets. Farther north, streets of heritage homes fill the Annex, leading to a remarkable piece of architecture.

Queen's Park and Midtown

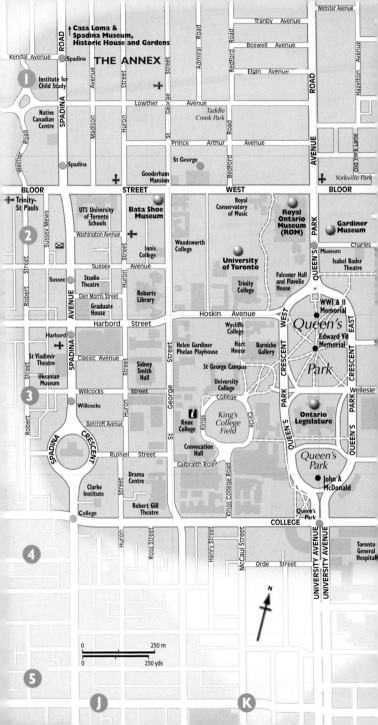

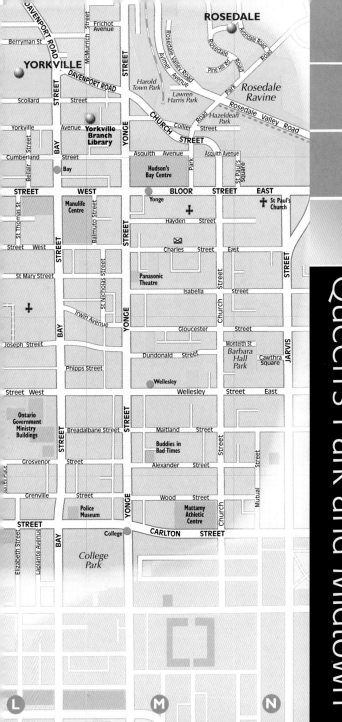

Bata Shoe Museum

Imelda Marcos would be in her element at this museum. Housed in a structure resembling a shoe box, there are more than 12,500 items in the displays of footwear past and present.

More than just shoes The main permanent exhibit traces the history of shoes from a footprint made 3.7 million years ago in Tanzania to the extraordinary shoes of today. The sheer variety of beautiful and truly striking footwear is amazing. Each display is set against an appropriate series of cutouts reflecting the particular period or geographic location. There are all kinds of ceremonial shoes: leather sandals with gilded images worn by the King of Kumasi in Ghana for state occasions; wedding shoes from various cultures; and lacquered and painted shoes worn to Shinto shrines

Clockwise from left: the hard-to-miss Bata Shoe Museum; interior staircase; exterior view; a pair of Elton John's shoes; sheepskin boots and moccasins; one of actress Lana Turner's sandals

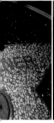

in Japan. The museum is a gold mine of little-known facts; for instance, that Elizabeth I was in part responsible for the foot problems caused by high heels because she popularized them in an attempt to make herself appear taller. The style was limited to the elite, hence the term "well-heeled." Toe-length was another indicator of social status; in England, in the mid-14th century, anyone earning less than 40 livres was not allowed to wear pointed toes, while a nobleman could wear shoes with toes 69cm (24in) long, and a prince could wear toes of any length.

The Walk of Fame This includes Picasso's mock zebra lace-ups, Elton John's 30cm (12in) high platform shoes, one of John Lennon's "Beatle Boots" from the early 1960s and Marilyn Monroe's red leather pumps.

THE BASICS

www.batashoemuseum.ca

➕ J2

✉ 327 Bloor Street West

☎ 416/979-7799

🕐 Mon–Wed, Fri–Sat 10–5, Thu 10–8, Sun 12–5

🚇 St. George

♿ Excellent

💵 Moderate; by donation Thu 5–8pm

❓ Lectures, guided tours, family events, folkloric events

Casa Loma

Interior views (below) and looking toward Casa Loma (right)

THE BASICS

www.casaloma.org

➕ Off map at J1

✉ 1 Austin Terrace at Davenport and Spadina Road

☎ 416/923-1171

🕐 House daily 9.30–5; gardens May–Oct daily 9.30–5. Last admission 4pm

🍴 Café

Ⓜ Dupont

♿ Good

💰 Expensive

❓ Self-guided audio tour; garden talks; special events

HIGHLIGHTS

● Great Hall
● Oak Room
● Conservatory
● View from the towers

TIPS

● Visitors with young children should be prepared to tackle staircases because the elevators can't take strollers.
● There's a charge for parking at Casa Loma.

A mix of 18th-century Scottish baronial and 20th-century Fox, Casa Loma is a rich man's folly. It cost $3.5 million to build, yet after real estate changes was valued at $27,305 only 10 years later.

Canadian-style splendor A magnificent and whimsical place with its Elizabethan chimneys, Rhenish turrets and secret passageways, Casa Loma is Sir Henry Pellatt's idea of what constituted European aristocratic splendor. Between 1911 and 1914 Pellatt created this fantasy home, importing Scottish stonemasons and Italian wood-carvers, then spending an additional $1.5 million furnishing the 98 rooms. A hammerbeam ceiling covers the 20m (66ft) high Great Hall; three artisans took three years to carve the paneling in the Oak Room; splendid bronze doors lead into a marble conservatory crowned with a stained-glass dome. Modern luxuries included an elevator, a private telephone system, marble swimming pool, 10,000-volume library, 15 baths and 5,000 electric lights. A tunnel runs out to the stables, where the horses, amid Spanish tile and mahogany, had their names displayed in 18-carat gold letters above the head of each stall.

The bubble bursts The son of a stockbroker, Pellatt went into the brokerage business after college, and amassed $17 million. Still in his twenties, he founded Toronto's first hydroelectric power company, but his wealth evaporated in 1920 when electric power was ruled a public utility. Pellatt eventually died penniless in 1939.

Gardiner Museum

Ceramic sculptures on display in the museum

THE BASICS

www.gardinermuseum.com
🖰 L2
✉ 111 Queen's Park
☎ 416/586-8080
🕐 Mon–Thu 10–6, Fri 10–9, Sat–Sun 10–5
🚇 Museum
♿ Very good
💵 Moderate; half-price Fri 4–9
❓ Tours, lectures

HIGHLIGHTS

● Olmec figures
● Smiling figures
● Majolica
● *Commedia dell'arte* figures
● Scent bottles

This outstanding museum is the only one in Canada dedicated to ceramic art. Its collections comprise more than 3,000 pieces, and include the Ancient Americas, Chinese, English, Italian, other European, Japanese and contemporary.

Colorful earthenware The marvelous collection of pre-Columbian pottery includes figures and vessels dating from 3000BC to the 16th century AD, ranging from Mexico to Peru. Among them are some remarkable pieces by the Olmecs, red clay Nayarit figures, Zacatecan-style male statuettes with mushroom-shape horns, smiling figures from Nopiloa, Los Cerro, or Isla de Sacrificios, fine orange and plumbate ware of the Mayans, and Aztec objects. The next great period of ceramic art is represented by colorful Italian majolica from the 15th and 16th centuries, and there is a selection of English tin-glazed earthenware, including familiar blue-and-white delftware.

Delicate porcelain The porcelain collection is extraordinary. It includes figures by Meissen's sculptor-potter Joachim Kändler and some prime examples of Sèvres. English porcelain is well represented, from the early softpaste pieces manufactured at Chelsea and Bow to the later bone china that was invented by Josiah Spode. The collection also features 120 figures from the *commedia dell'arte* and 100 mid-18th-century scent bottles, with examples ranging from early Meissen to highly decorated rococo versions from various sources.

Ontario Legislature

Most parliamentary institutions deliver great entertainment, and the Ontario Provincial legislature is no exception, with the 107 members heckling and cheering as they debate and pass laws. The highlight of any day in the chamber is question time.

Parliamentary session In this impressive four-story chamber the laws affecting 13 million Ontarians are passed. On a dais sits the Speaker, who presides over the house. To the right sits the Government; to the left, the Opposition. In the center is the Clerks' table, with the mace. Behind the Clerks' table is a smaller table for Hansard record-keepers. On the steps of the dais sit the Legislative Pages, who run errands in the house. Above the Speaker is the press gallery. Sessions are opened and closed by the Lieutenant Governor representing Queen Elizabeth II.

Architectural and historical grandeur Even if the house is not sitting you can tour the building, a massive Romanesque Revival structure of reddish-brown sandstone, opened in 1893. A grand staircase lined with portraits of Ontario premiers sweeps up to the chamber above. An enormous stained-glass ceiling-window lights the East Wing, where the premier has his office. The west lobby has mosaic floors, and Italian marble columns in the beaux-arts style, with carved capitals. On the ground level are exhibits, including the provincial mace, which was stolen by the Americans during the 1812 War and returned only in 1934.

THE BASICS

www.ontla.on.ca
⊞ K3
✉ Queen's Park
☎ 416/325-7500
🕐 Victoria Day Weekend–Labour Day daily 8–4; rest of year Mon–Fri 8.30–6
🍴 Cafeteria, dining room
🚇 Queen's Park, Museum
♿ Good
💷 Free
❓ Public gallery viewing when parliament is in session

HIGHLIGHTS

● Chamber of the Legislature
● Question time
● Stained-glass ceiling in the East Wing
● The mace

Royal Ontario Museum

HIGHLIGHTS

- Dinosaurs
- Stair of Wonders
- Spirit House
- China Galleries
- Middle East and South Asia
- The Americas Gallery

TIPS

- Discounted admission rates on Fridays starting at 4.30pm.
- School groups tend to visit in the morning.

As one of North America's great museums and Canada's largest, the Royal Ontario Museum (ROM) opened in 1914 and continues to be one of the main attractions in the city today.

Michael Lee-Chin Crystal Ever controversial, the Crystal addition built in 2007 literally bursts out of the century-old walls of the original museum in great prisms that tower over Bloor Street, enabling passersby to look up and see exhibits in the halls above. Inside, seven galleries have crazy angles and sweeping curves and are bathed in natural light. A fine-dining restaurant has incredible views. Threading up through the building is the Stair of Wonders, highlighting the museum's more unusual exhibits.

Clockwise from left: entrance to the museum; a totem inside the museum; a highly decorated ceiling; detail of an arch above the windows at the entrance; bronze seated Buddha on display; outside the gallery

The collections The ROM has almost 6 million objects in its varied collections, which incorporate world cultures and natural history. The Chinese collections are particularly oustanding, and include galleries devoted to temple art, sculpture, decorative arts and other historic objects. Canada is represented in the excellent Sigmund Samuel and Daphne Cockwell galleries, the latter focusing on First Peoples' culture and art. Other exhibitions range from ancient European civilizations to Japanese ceramics.

For children Most popular with children—and many adults—is the world-class collection of dinosaur skeletons and fossils, and the bat exhibit, which includes a walk-through bat cave diorama. Young visitors are also enthralled by the hands-on galleries, including a digital suite.

THE BASICS

www.rom.on.ca

🚫 K2

✉ 100 Queen's Park

☎ 416/586-8000

🕐 Mon–Thu, Sat–Sun 10–5.30, Fri 10–8.30

🍴 Food Cafe

🚇 St. George, Museum

♿ Excellent

💲 Moderate

University of Toronto

Exterior (below left) and the Great Hall of Hart House (below right); the Humanities wing (opposite)

THE BASICS

www.utoronto.ca

✚ K2

✉ West of Queen's Park

☎ 416/978-2011

🍴 Gallery Grill in Hart House and numerous cafeterias in campus buildings

🚇 Museum or Queen's Park

🚋 506 Carlton streetcar

♿ Good

🎫 Free

❓ Tours year-round

HIGHLIGHTS

● Hart House
● Knox College Circle
● Robarts Library
● Justina M. Barnicke Gallery

Important scientific discoveries have been made at this venerable institution, most notably insulin. The university also numbers many world-famous names among its past students and teachers.

Famous alumni and remarkable research Canada's largest university was founded in 1827. Its scientific achievements include work that led to the development of the chemical laser; the first electronic heart pacemaker; and some groundbreaking discoveries in genetics. Notable alumni include authors Margaret Atwood, Farley Mowat and Stephen Leacock; figures from the movie world Atom Egoyan, Norman Jewison and Donald Sutherland; opera singers Teresa Stratas and Maureen Forrester; and prime ministers Mackenzie King and Lester Pearson.

Gothic and modern Stroll around the main St. George campus to view the mixture of architecture. On Hoskin Avenue see Wycliffe and Trinity colleges, the first a monument of redbrick Romanesque Revival and the second a Gothic complex with chapel and eye-catching gardens. Around the corner on Devonshire Place, Massey College is a 1960s building. The heart of the university is Hart House, modeled on Magdalen College, Oxford. See the collection of Canadian art in the Justina M. Barnicke Gallery in the west wing. South of Hart House is the Romanesque Revival University College, with an arts center in the Laidlaw Building. King's College Circle passes by several other stately university buildings.

Yorkville

Relaxing in an outdoor Park on Cumberland Street

THE BASICS

🔲 L1
✉ Bloor Street West, Davenport Road, and Yonge Street
Ⓑ Bloor Yonge

HIGHLIGHTS

● Royal Ontario Museum
● Village of Yorkville Park
● Joso's seafood restaurant

From a 19th-century residential suburb lined with Victorian-style homes to bohemian cultural centre in the 1960s to the upscale shopping district that it is today, the Yorkville neighbourhood (locally known as Bloor-Yorkville) is as chic as it gets for Toronto.

Home to the stars Comparable to New York's Fifth Avenue and LA's Rodeo Drive, the Yorkville neighborhood is often dubbed the Mink Mile. The area's history, however, is quite humble: starting off as a small village outside of the city in the 1850s, and then later becoming a sort of Haight-Ashbury in the 1960s when it was home to local talents Joni Mitchell and Neil Young. Famous literary figures such as Margaret Atwood and Gwendolyn MacEwen also started out here.

Exclusive stores galore Now an exclusive shopping district, bound by Bloor Street West, Davenport Road and Yonge Steet, this area is far more glitz and glamor than beads and bandanas. Plush hotels alongside swank art galleries, expensive condos, and luxury shops and restaurants keep Torontonians and visitors enthralled, albeit with thinner wallets when they leave. Exclusive fashion stores include Burberry, Tiffany & Co., Prada, Louis Vuitton and many more world-famous designer names. Flagship stores for upscale department stores, such as Holt Renfrew and Harry Rosen, are also here. There are some mid-range shops as well, including Banana Republic, American Apparel, and Roots.

More to See

ROSEDALE

If you truly want to escape the city then visit Rosedale, Toronto's most affluent and elegant neighborhoods, with large, beautiful homes owned by the city's movers and shakers. Many of the buildings, which mostly date from the mid-19th century to the 1920s, are listed Heritage Properties, and are set on large, landscaped lots around pleasant leafy streets. It's no accident that some of Toronto's most upscale shopping abuts Rosedale, in the Yorkville area (▷ 86). The district makes for a pleasant stroll and there are plenty of places to stop for a drink while soaking up the sheer luxury of it all.

🚹 M1 🚇 Rosedale

SPADINA MUSEUM: HISTORIC HOUSE AND GARDENS

www.toronto.ca

Just along the road from over-the-top Casa Loma (▷ 78–79), this fine mansion, with its original furnishings and gas lights, was once at the heart of an estate with its own golf course. After an entertaining introductory film, there's an excellent guided tour that really brings the Austin family to life, with anecdotes and pointers to personal possessions of the family that still dot the rooms. Afterward, you can take a stroll in the lovely gardens.

🚹 Off map at J1 ✉ 285 Spadina Road
☎ 416/392-6910 🕐 Apr–Labour Day Tue–Sun and holiday Mon 12–5; Sep–Jan Tue–Fri 12–4, Sat–Sun and Thanksgiving Mon 12–5; Jan–Mar Sat–Sun 12–5 🚇 Dupont
♿ Good ✋ Inexpensive

YORKVILLE BRANCH LIBRARY

www.torontopubliclibrary.ca

Built in 1907 as the first of four libraries for the Toronto Public Library system, the Yorkville Branch is in classical Beaux Arts style and is now the system's oldest library. Renovated in 1978 and 2010, the library is home to a local history and theater collection, and an Art Exhibit Space.

🚹 M1 ☎ 416/393-7660 🕐 Mon–Thu 9–8.30, Fri–Sat 9–5 🚇 Bloor-Yonge

Spadina House

Midtown Hits

Yet another facet of Toronto: the stately buildings of parliament and academia, the ROM, and upscale shopping in Yorkville.

DISTANCE: 3km (1.8 miles) **ALLOW:** 2 hours

START

ONTARIO PARLIAMENT
➕ L7 🚇 Union Square

1 Turn your back to the facade of the Ontario Provincial Parliament Buildings, walk south to College Street and turn right. At King's College Road take another right and walk through the university campus.

2 Take King's College Circle west to Tower Road. En route, on your left, will be University College opposite the Stewart Observatory.

3 Proceed northeast to Hart House, pause for a meal at the Gallery Grill, and then visit Soldier's Memorial Tower. Turn right along Hoskin Avenue to Trinity College and then walk east toward Queen's Park.

4 Left on Avenue Road, going north past the Royal Ontario Museum and the Gardiner Museum. Make a right on fashionable Bloor Street, then head left on Yonge Street to Cumberland Street and walk west.

END

BLOOR-YONGE
➕ L8 🚇 Queens Park

8 Continue to Yonge. Turn right and cross the street to the Toronto Reference Library and walk south to the Bloor-Yonge subway stop.

7 Come back out the way you went in and browse through the galleries on Hazelton Avenue. Backtrack to Yorkville Avenue and go left along it to Bay Street. Cross Bay and note the old Firehall and the Yorkville Branch Library, both on the left.

6 Cross Yorkville and go down Hazelton Lane to the Hazelton Lanes Complex, where contemporary designer stores can be found, along with the vast Whole Foods Market—a superb organic food emporium.

5 You are now in the trendy shopping area of Yorkville. Turn down Old York Lane to Yorkville Avenue.

Shopping

ALL THE BEST FINE FOODS

www.allthebestfinefoods.com
Take a leaf out of the book of Rosedale's residents and stop here to buy breads, salads, entrées, jams, relishes, sauces and cheeses.
➕ K5 ✉ 1101 Yonge Street ☎ 416/928-3330 Ⓜ Rosedale

CRAFT ONTARIO

www.craftontario.com
This is a prime place to purchase the latest and best in Canadian crafts by named artists, as well as Inuit and Native Canadian art.
➕ J6 ✉ 118 Cumberland Street ☎ 416/921-1721 Ⓜ Bay

DISH COOKING STUDIO

www.dishcookingstudio.com
This Yabu Pushelberg-designed studio combines cooking school, café and retail store. You'll also find a wide range of gorgeous kitchenware—the creations of Trish Magwood, host of Food Network's *Party Dish*—tableware, cookbooks, plus spices, oils, teas and other ingredients.
➕ H5 ✉ 390 Dupont Street ☎ 416/920-5559 Ⓜ Dupont

GRIGORIAN

www.grigorian.com
This is a store for the devoted music lover. It contains a stunning collection of classical music and jazz CDs.
➕ J6 ✉ 70 Yorkville Avenue ☎ 416/922-6477 Ⓜ Bloor-Yonge

HARRY ROSEN

www.harryrosen.com
Five floors of fashions for men, including all the top men's designers—Armani, Valentino, Calvin Klein and Hugo Boss.
➕ J6 ✉ 82 Bloor Street West ☎ 416/972-0556 Ⓜ Bloor-Yonge or Bay

HOLT RENFREW

www.holtrenfrew.com
Canada's answer to Harvey Nichols. Three floors of designer fashion, a hairdressing salon, spa, perfumes, and a café.
➕ J6 ✉ 50 Bloor Street West ☎ 416/922-2333 Ⓜ St. George

M0851

www.m0851.com
Minimalist, high quality leather accessories, bags, coats and outerwear for men and women. All are designed and manufactured in Montreal.
➕ K1 ✉ 38 Avenue Road ☎ 416/920-4001 Ⓜ St. George

REFLECTIONS VINTAGE & ANTIQUES

A fun store selling a wide range of costumes for almost any occasion, but there is also some antique jewelry, porcelain, glass and bronzes for sale. A real treasure trove.
➕ M2 ✉ 676 Yonge Street ☎ 416/944-0333 Ⓜ Wellesley

ROLO

www.rolostore.com
If it's unique gadgets and gifts you are looking for, head to tiny, friendly Rolo for a wide assortment of novelty items, most at under $25.
➕ L1 ✉ 24 Bellair Street ☎ 416/920-0100 Ⓜ Bay

SILVERBRIDGE

www.silverbridge.com
Marvelously sculptured pieces of sterling silver. Necklaces, bracelets, rings and earrings for women, plus cuff links, money clips and key holders for men, all beautifully crafted. Prices range from $60 to $1,600.
➕ J6 ✉ 162 Cumberland Street ☎ 416/923-2591 Ⓜ Bay

STOLLERY'S

www.stollerys.com
Long-established store selling men and women's clothes with a distinct British flavor.
➕ K6 ✉ 1 Bloor Street West ☎ 416/922-6173 Ⓜ Bloor-Yonge

WILLIAM ASHLEY CHINA

www.williamashley.com
Stocking all the great names in china and in glass (Kosta Boda, Waterford, Baccarat).
➕ J6 ✉ 55 Bloor Street West ☎ 416/964-2900 Ⓜ Bloor-Yonge

Entertainment and Nightlife

BA BA LÚU
www.babaluu.com
A sophisticated venue in Yorkville that's popular for its salsa and Latin food.
🔶 L1 ✉ 136 Yorkville Avenue, Lower Level
☎ 416/515-0587 🚇 Bay

BUDDIES IN BAD TIMES THEATRE
www.buddiesinbadtimes.com
This is the premier gay theater in Canada but it has also nurtured many contemporary straight writers. On the cutting edge, it delivers theater that challenges social boundaries. Extra draws are Tallulah's Cabaret (very popular Fri and Sat) and the bar.
🔶 M3 ✉ 12 Alexander Street ☎ 416/975-8555 🚇 College, Wellesley

DBAR
www.dbartoronto.com
An elegant cocktail lounge with a tempting appetizer menu. Expect celebrity spotting here, excellent service, and don't forget to check out the terrace.
🔶 L1 ✉ Four Seasons Hotel, 60 Yorkville Avenue
☎ 416/964-0411 🚇 Bay

FREE TIMES CAFÉ
www.freetimescafe.com
Go to hear the folk acoustic entertainment. Monday is open house, so bring your instrument and sign up at 7pm.
🔶 H4 ✉ 320 College Street between Major and Roberts ☎ 416/967-1078 🚋 507 Carlton, College streetcars

HART HOUSE THEATRE
www.harthouse.ca
The performing arts venue of the University of Toronto showcases Canada's talent in a range of productions.
🔶 K3 ✉ 7 Hart House Circle, University of Toronto
☎ 416/978-8849 🚇 Queen's Park, Museum

LEE'S PALACE
www.leespalace.com
Venue for the latest in rock music, including

GAY TORONTO
To get a fix on the scene, pick up *Xtra!* or go to **Glad Day Bookshop** (🔶 K6 ✉ 598a Yonge Street ☎ 416/961-4161, www.gladdaybookshop.com). Also check these websites: www.dailyxtra.com; and www.seetorontonow.com/toronto-diversity. The area around the Church Street and Wellesley Street intersection has joined the ranks of Toronto's "neighborhoods" as the Church & Wellesley Gay Village, with lots of clubs and bars, including **Woody's** (🔶 K7 ✉ 467 Church Street ☎ 416/972-0887); **Byzantium** (🔶 M3 ✉ 499 Church Street ☎ 416/922-3859); **Statlers** (🔶 M3 ✉ 487 Church Street ☎ 416/922-0487) and **Crews & Tangos** (🔶 M3 ✉ 508 Church Street ☎ 647/349-7469).

up-and-coming British groups. Home to local alternative bands. Dance bar with DJ.
🔶 H2 ✉ 529 Bloor Street West ☎ 416/532-1598 🚇 Bathurst

PEGASUS BAR
www.pegasusonchurch.com
This lively place in Toronto's gay village is for everyone, with music and dancing that's less frantic than in the nearby clubs. You can also play pool and darts, or just enjoy a drink.
🔶 M3 ✉ 489B Church Street ☎ 416/927-8832 🚇 Wellesley

PHOENIX CONCERT THEATRE
Mos Def, Queensrÿche and Noah and the Whale have played here. Dance on weekends in an extravagant Egyptian-Greek fantasy set.
🔶 N3 ✉ 410 Sherbourne Street ☎ 416/323-1251 🚇 Wellesley or College

TRANZAC
www.tranzac.org
The Toronto Australia New Zealand Club is a nonprofit venue promoting music, theater and the arts in both the Main Hall and the Southern Cross Lounge. There's something on most evenings, including folk, jazz and indie bands, some with no cover charge.
🔶 H2 ✉ 292 Brunswick Avenue ☎ 416/923-8137 🚇 Spadina

Restaurants

PRICES

Prices are approximate, based on a 3-course meal for one person.

$$$$	over $80
$$$	$60–$80
$$	$35–$60
$	under $35

BLOOR STREET DINER ($)

www.bloorstreetdiner.com
Serving shoppers and late-nighters, it combines an espresso bar, a rotisserie where meat and fish are prepared in Provençal style and a café-terracce in summer.
✚ L2 ⊠ 55 Bloor Street West in the Manulife Centre ☎ 416/928-3105 🕐 Daily 11.30am–midnight (till 2am Fri–Sat) 🚇 Bay or Bloor-Yonge

COMO EN CASA ($)

www.comoencasa.ca
Welcoming, easy-going Mexican restaurant serving generous portions.
✚ M3 ⊠ 565 Yonge Street ☎ 647/748-6666 🕐 Mon–Fri 11am–9pm, Sat noon–9pm 🚇 Wellesley

CRÈME BRASSERIE ($$)

www.cremebrasserie.com
Romantic and classy with a courtyard patio, serving fine French food such as steak tartare, smoked duck, and fricassee of rabbit. Fabulous desserts.
✚ L1 ⊠ 162 Cumberland Street ☎ 416/962-7363 🕐 Mon 5–11, Tue–Sat 11.30–11 🚇 Bay

FIERAMOSCA ($$)

www.fieramoscatoronto.com
This trattoria delivers good Southern Italian dishes. The leafy patio is perfect for sunnier days. There's also a private dining room with a terrace upstairs.
✚ K1 ⊠ 36A Prince Arthur Avenue ☎ 416/323-0636 🕐 Mon–Fri 11–3, Sat–Sun 5–11 🚇 St. George

FUTURE BISTRO ($)

www.futurebistro.ca
European-style cafeteria, beloved for its large portions of goulash and schnitzel sandwiches.
✚ H3 ⊠ 483 Bloor Street West ☎ 416/922-5875 🕐 Daily 8am–1am, Fri–Sat till 2am 🚇 Spadina or Bathurst

JOSO'S ($$)

www.josos.com
The best place for fresh fish in Toronto. Select your own fish from the tray and it will be grilled, steamed, poached, or cooked to order. The calamari are legendary.
✚ Off map at L1 ⊠ 202 Davenport Road (just east of Avenue Road) ☎ 416/925-1903 🕐 Lunch Mon–Fri; dinner Mon–Sat 🚇 Bay 🚌 Bus 6

AGE LIMITS

The legal drinking age in Ontario is 19, and young people should be prepared to show photo ID because entry and/or alcohol service can be refused.

MORTON'S ($$$)

www.mortons.com
A superb steakhouse that serves United States Department of Agriculture rated prime beef.
✚ K1 ⊠ Park Hyatt Hotel, 4 Avenue Road ☎ 416/925-0648 🕐 Dinner daily 🚇 Bay or Museum

MUSEUM TAVERN ($)

www.museumtavern.ca
American pub food with a welcome twist: elk sliders, duck buns, beef short rib poutine, truffled perogies. Some classic menu items too. There's a good view of the Royal Ontario Museum from the patio.
✚ K2 ⊠ 208 Bloor Street West ☎ 416/920-0110 🕐 Daily 11.30–late 🚇 St. George

SOUTHERN ACCENT ($)

www.southernaccent.com
In Markham Village, with a canopy-covered brick patio. Gumbo, jambalaya, blackened fish and other Louisiana dishes.
✚ G2 ⊠ 595 Markham Street ☎ 416/536-3211 🕐 Dinner Tue–Sun 🚇 Bathurst

WOW SUSHI ($)

Tiny sushi restaurant owned by two brothers. Skilled chefs create behind the counter. Try the Rainbow roll or the Japango roll.
✚ M2 ⊠ 11 Charles Street West ☎ 416/923-1888 🕐 Daily 11–10 🚇 Yonge

It is worth discovering some of the excellent attractions of the Greater Toronto area and beyond. You will find first-class culture, delightful and lively heritage towns and one of the greatest wonders of the natural world.

Kortright Centre
for Conservation

McMichael
Canadian Art
Collection

Canada's
Wonderland

RUTHERFORD ROAD

Rutherford

RICHMOND
HILL

Langstaff

LANGSTAFF ROAD

*Don
Valley*

VAUGHAN

*Humber
Valley
Park*

HIGHWAY 7

WOODBRIDGE

407 TOLL HIGHWAY

THORNHILL

STEELES AVENUE

Black Creek
Pioneer Village

York University

*Ross Lord
Park*

East Don

*Old
Cummer*

FINCH AVENUE WEST

SHEPPARD AVENUE NORTH YORK

*Don
Valley*

*Downsview
Park*

*Earl Bales
Park*

Oriole

Toronto Pearson
Int Airport

Etobicoke North

WILSON AVENUE

401

*Edwards
Gardens*

African
Lion Safari

Weston

LAWRENCE AVENUE WEST

*Sunnybrook
Park*

ETOBICOKE

EGLINTON AVENUE WEST

YORK

Ontario
Science
Centre

*Smythe
Park*

ST CLAIR AVENUE WEST

Todmorden
Mills

*Humber
Valley
Park*

Bloor

BLOOR STREET WEST

EAST YORK

Kipling

High Park &
Colborne Lodge

TORONTO

QUEEN STREET WEST

QUEEN STREET EAST

QEW

Mimico

Exhibition

Toronto Union
Station

*Humber
Bay*

GARDINER EXPRESSWAY

LAKESHORE

*Humber
Bay Park*

*Western
Beaches*

*Toronto
Harbour*

*Long
Branch
Park*

Toronto Island
Airport

*Leslie
Street Spit*

*Toronto
Islands*

Tommy
Thompson
Park

Lake Ontario

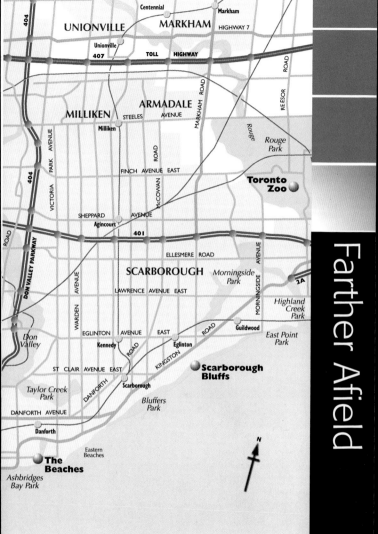

16TH AVENUE

Centennial

Markham

UNIONVILLE

MARKHAM

HIGHWAY 7

Unionville

407   TOLL   HIGHWAY

MARKHAM ROAD

REESOR ROAD

404

ARMADALE

MILLIKEN   STEELES   AVENUE

Milliken

Rouge

Rouge Park

PARK AVENUE

McCOWAN ROAD

FINCH   AVENUE   EAST

VICTORIA

404

Toronto Zoo

SHEPPARD   AVENUE

ROAD

Agincourt

401

DON VALLEY PARKWAY

ELLESMERE   ROAD

MORNINGSIDE AVENUE

SCARBOROUGH   Morningside Park

WARDEN   AVENUE

LAWRENCE   AVENUE   EAST

Highland Creek Park

2A

EGLINTON   AVENUE   EAST

Guildwood

East Point Park

Don Valley

Kennedy

DANFORTH ROAD

Eglinton

KINGSTON ROAD

ROAD

ST CLAIR   AVENUE   EAST

Scarborough

Scarborough Bluffs

Taylor Creek Park

Bluffers Park

DANFORTH   AVENUE

Danforth

Eastern Beaches

N

The Beaches

Ashbridges Bay Park

Lake Ontario

Black Creek Pioneer Village

TOP 25

Inside the weaver's shop (left); traditional general store (right)

THE BASICS

www.blackcreek.ca
🔳 Off map to northwest
✉ 1000 Murray Ross Parkway, North York
☎ 416/736-1733
🕐 May–Jun Mon–Fri 9.30–4, Sat–Sun 11–5; Jul–Sep Mon–Fri 10–5, Sat–Sun 11–5; Oct–Dec Mon–Fri 9.30–4, Sat–Sun 11.30–4.30. Closed Jan–Apr
🍴 Restaurant and snack bar
🚇 Jane subway then 35 bus; Finch subway then 60 bus
♿ Good
✋ Moderate

HIGHLIGHTS

● Coopering
● Tinsmithing
● Flour milling
● Heritage gardens
● Laskay Emporium and Post Office
● Half Way House

This living-history park authentically re-creates life in a 19th-century Ontario village. Leave behind the stresses of modern times and step back into the past to find out about existence in a pioneer community.

Family farm Black Creek is built around the Stong family farm—their first log house (1816), smokehouse and barn (1825), and a second clapboard home that they built in 1832. Even the sheep and hogs are imported English breeds that would have been familiar to the 19th-century pioneers.

Village life The village consists of 40 mid-19th-century buildings. Seeds are sold at the Laskay Emporium store, along with old-fashioned candy and brooms made in the village. Half Way House Inn and Restaurant (it stood halfway between York and Scarborough) is a stagecoach tavern. Loaves are baked here daily in the old hearth oven. These surroundings are brought to life by the artisans, who take delight in passing on their skills and knowledge. The cooper hunches over the barrel stove compressing staves to make barrels and pails held together without a single nail. Others demonstrate tinsmithing, weaving, cabinetmaking, blacksmithing, clockmaking and printing. Dickson's Hill School is a one-room schoolhouse that has separate entrances for boys and girls. The gardens include a herb garden with 42 herbs, the weaver's shop dye garden with plants, such as bloodroot (red), sunflowers (yellow) and woad (blue), and a medicinal garden.

The cafeteria and exterior of the building housing the collection

McMichael Canadian Art Collection

Tom Thomson and the artists known as the Group of Seven took their easels north and painted what they saw, revealing the northern wilderness to the rest of the world. Their revolutionary works are now displayed in a woodland setting.

Artist by artist The permanent collection chronicles the development of the Group of Seven. The works of each artist are hung together so that viewers can see how the individuals evolved. All the favorites are here: the brilliantly colored canvases of Lake Superior by Alexander Young Jackson; Algonquin Park as seen by Tom Thomson; the rural villages depicted by Alfred Joseph Casson; the Killarney Provincial Park rendered by Franklin Carmichael; the starkly beautiful icebergs captured by Lawren Harris; portraits of British Columbia by Frederick Horsman Varley; and the portrayal of northwestern forests and First Nations villages by Emily Carr. In one gallery, a series of paintings portrays the Seven working outdoors. The most appealing depicts Franklin Carmichael sketching at Grace Lake in 1935, perching in front of an easel wrapped in a heavy parka.

First Nations and Inuit art Paintings, drawings, prints and sculptures by contemporary First Nations and Inuit artists—Norval Morrisseau, Daphne Odjig, Alex Janvier, Bill Reid—are displayed in changing shows drawn from the gallery's permanent collection. Fine Inuit sculptures and other crafts complete this excellent collection.

THE BASICS

www.mcmichael.com
🞧 Off map to northwest
✉ 10365 Islington Avenue, Kleinburg
☎ 905/893-1121 or 1-888/213-1121
🕐 Daily 10–5
🍴 Cafeteria
🚇 Yonge–University–Spadina to bus 60, then bus 13
♿ Good
💲 Moderate
❓ Daily tours at 12.30pm and 2pm

HIGHLIGHTS

● Emily Carr's *Corner of Kitwancool Village*
● Lawren Harris's *Mt. Lefroy*
● J. E. H. MacDonald's *Forest Wilderness*
● A. Y. Jackson's *First Snow*
● Tom Thomson's *Wood Interior, Winter*
● Arthur Lismer's *Bright Land*
● F. H. Varley's *Night Ferry*
● First Nations art
● Inuit sculpture

Canada's Wonderland

HIGHLIGHTS

● Behemoth
● Splash Works
● White Water Canyon
● Backlot Stunt Coaster
● Halloween events

TIPS

● Buying tickets online is cheaper; the two-day pass is a good value, and late afternoon admission is almost half price.
● You can't picnic inside the park, but there's an area outside the front gate.

Roller coaster addicts will revel in Canada's Wonderland because it contains no less than 16 coasters. The park has more than 65 rides and 200 attractions—adding new thrillers every year to keep the locals coming back.

Gut-wrenchers The latest ride is the dark Wonder Mountain's Guardian coaster, a 4D interactive ride. The Behemoth is the fastest coaster in Canada at 125km/h (78mph), while Shockwave spins and loops riders through 360 degrees and at a height of 21m (70ft). The daredevil Drop Tower takes riders 70m (230ft) up into the air and then drops them in a 96kph (60mph) free fall. The Xtreme Skyflyer, lifting riders 45m (150ft) into the air, delivers all the thrills and sensations of skydiving and hang-gliding.

Clockwise from left: Levithian—the tallest ride in the park; the free-fall Drop Zone ride; the Psyclone ride in full swing; the waterpark area of Wonderland, Splash Works; the Vortex ride twists and turns over the water; visitors can ride 16 coasters in the park

A few other favorites include the tallest ride in the park, Leviathan, and the Backlot Stunt Coaster.

Water plus Perfect for a hot day, Splash Works is the 8ha (20-acre) water park, with an extra-large wave pool generating white caps, and 18 water slides, including one with a 120m (400ft) drop in the dark. There's also a fun aquatic jungle gym that's suitable for younger or more timid children.

Gentler fun There are lots of gentler rides too, including an antique carousel, while younger children will have plenty of fun in Kidzville and Planet Snoopy. There's also a Peanuts 500 raceway with two-seater cars. Live shows include Snoopy's Symphony of Water, Charlie Brown's Pirate Adventure, and fireworks in the summer.

THE BASICS

www.canadaswonderland.com

➕ Off map to northwest

✉ 9580 Jane Street Vaughan. Take Hwy 400 to Rutherford Road

☎ 905/832-8131

🕐 Early May–early Oct daily. Hours vary throughout the season

🍴 Many outlets

🚇 Yorkdale or York Mills then GO bus

🚌 165A

♿ Few

💲 Expensive (One Price Passport). Additional fees for some events

Ontario Science Centre

HIGHLIGHTS

- Human Body Hall
- Science Arcade
- Living Earth
- Space Hall
- TELUSCAPE
- KidSpark
- Cloud

TIPS

- Look for staff wearing lab coats—they are there to help and explain.
- You save money on combined tickets if you decide to see an IMAX movie.

This leading interactive science museum designs and builds exhibits for others around the world. It also has one of the few meteorites from Mars on public display in Canada.

Hands-on TELUSCAPE is an outdoor area with plenty of interactive exhibits in the center's forecourt, connecting science to nature and the landscape. The central FUNtain enables you to make music by interrupting the water flow. Designed with teens and young adults in mind, the Weston Family Innovation Centre provides "experiences" rather than exhibits, challenging young people to look at things differently and develop their skills, from making unusual music and art to learning how to read the body language of a liar. KidSpark provides similar fun for the

A vast playground of science, visitors can trace the developement of technology (left); interactive displays engage visitors to the Science Centre (below)

under-8s, with water play, learning math and nutrition while shopping, music and art exhibits and other activities.

Old favorites The Science Arcade is where you'll find the popular hair-raising electricity demonstration, the distorted room, pedal power and puzzles and illusions. Living Earth has a re-created rain forest and other wonders, while in the Human Body hall you can see how you'll look as you age. The Sport hall combines athletic activities with virtual sport experiences.

Movie magic The Omnimax Theatre has a 24m (79ft) dome screen with digital wraparound sound that creates the illusion of being right in the movie. You sit in a tilted-back seat and watch a screen 10 times larger than most IMAX formats.

THE BASICS

www.ontarioscience
centre.ca

➕ Off map to northeast

✉ 770 Don Mills Road, North York at Eglinton

☎ 416/696-1000 or 1-888/696-1110

🕐 Daily 10–5

🍴 Food court, cafés

🚇 Pape then bus 25 north; Eglinton then bus 34 east

♿ Very good

💲 Expensive

Toronto Zoo

This polar bear and gorilla are among the 5,000 animals housed at the zoo

THE BASICS

www.torontozoo.com
🔾 Off map to northeast
✉ 361A Old Finch Avenue, Scarborough
☎ 416/392-5929
🕐 May–Aug 9–7, Sep–Apr 9.30–4.30 (till 6pm on weekends and holidays from Sep–Nov)
🍴 Various outlets
🚇 Kennedy then Scarborough bus 86A going east
🚻 Very good
💰 Expensive
❓ "Meet the Keeper" program at various times and venues throughout the day

HIGHLIGHTS

● Canadian Domain
● Giant pandas
● Tundra Trek
● Gorilla Rainforest
● Great Barrier Reef

TIP

● Admission is discounted during the low season, Nov–Apr.

The 5,000 or so animals here representing more than 460 species, have more freedom than many in similar institutions. Even their pavilions re-create their natural environment as much as possible.

Australasia, Eurasia and the Americas
Inspired by the San Diego Zoo, the 287ha (710 acres) are organized around seven pavilions and outdoor paddocks. Inside each pavilion, habitats and climates are replicated using flora, fauna, birds and butterflies. The Australasia Pavilion includes a new 7m (23ft) long Great Barrier Reef tank, circular column tanks for jellyfish and other sea creatures, and an Outback area. The nearby Eurasia Outdoor Exhibits includes the Siberian tiger, snow leopard and yak. The Americas Pavilion includes alligators, black widow spiders, boa constrictors, Mojave desert sidewinders and pink-toed tarantulas. The Tundra Trek showcases polar bears, snowy owls, arctic foxes, and arctic wolves.

Africa and the Indo-Malayan Pavilion
The Africa Pavilion houses the Gorilla Rainforest exhibit. Outdoors, you can go on safari observing zebra, lion, giraffe, ostrich, cheetah, hyena, white rhinos and antelope. The orangutan and white-handed gibbon entertain in the Indo-Malaya Pavilion, along with hornbill and reticulated python. Near the pavilion are the Sumatran tigers, Indian rhinoceros, lion-tailed macaque and, in the Malayan Woods Pavilion, clouded leopard. In the Canadian Domain are a large herd of wood bison plus grizzly bear, lynx and cougar.

More to See

AFRICAN LION SAFARI
www.lionsafari.com
It's not just lions here. More than 1,000 animals are kept in spacious drive-through reserves, including rhinos, primates, giraffes, zebras and elephants. There are boat and train rides, elephant bathing and birds of prey flying demonstrations and a jungle playground and wet play area.

➕ Off map to southwest ✉ 1386 Cooper Road, Flamborough. Take Hwy 401 to Hwy 6 south ☎ 519/623-2620 🕐 May–Aug 10–5.30, Sep–Oct 10–4 🍴 Cafeteria/snack bar 💲 Expensive

THE BEACHES
At the eastern end of Queen Street, this is the district favored by baby boomers, attracted to the small-town atmosphere, the boardwalk along the lake and attractive Victorian homes along tree-shaded streets. Quirky stores, restaurants, cafés and antiques stores add interest.

➕ Off map to east 🚌 Queen Street East streetcar

EDWARDS GARDENS
This garden is popular in good weather, especially when the rhododendrons are in flower.

➕ Off map to northeast ✉ 755 Lawrence Avenue East ☎ 416/392-8188 🕐 Daily dawn–dusk 🚇 Eglinton then Lawrence East bus 54, 54A 🚭 Good 💲 Free

HIGH PARK & COLBORNE LODGE
www.highpark.org
Colborne Lodge (1836–37) and the surrounding 161ha (400 acres) were donated to the city in 1873. The park has a small zoo and adventure playground. People come to cycle, jog, stroll, picnic and swim in the pool. In winter Grenadier Pond is a skating rink.

➕ Off map to west ✉ Bloor Street West and Parkside Drive ☎ 416/392-6916, 416/392-6916 Colborne Lodge 🕐 High Park: May–Aug Tue–Sun 12–5; Sep Sat–Sun 12–5; Oct–Dec Tue–Sun 12–4; mid-Jan to Apr Fri–Sun 12–4 Colborne Lodge: daily dawn–dusk. 🚇 High Park 🚌 501 Queen streetcar 🚭 Good; Colborne Lodge none 💲 Park: free; Colborne Lodge: inexpensive

Giraffes and zebras examine a visitor to the African Lion Safari

Playing volleyball at The Beaches

KORTRIGHT CENTRE FOR CONSERVATION

www.kortright.org

The Kortright Centre is a conservation and environmental facility, where the Power Trip Trail threads for 1.6 km (1 mile) between fascinating and educational demonstrations on energy efficiency, renewable energy and sustainable building methods. More information can be gleaned from various projects on site. You can also enjoy more than 16km (10 miles) of hiking trails through forest and marshland.

➕ Off map to northwest ✉ 9550 Pine Valley Drive, Woodbridge ☎ 905/832-2289 ⏰ Daily 10–4 🍴 Café ♿ Good 💷 Inexpensive

SCARBOROUGH BLUFFS

Created by erosion, the dramatic Scarborough Bluffs line a 15km (9.3-mile) stretch of lakeshore to the east of Toronto, rising to more than 90m (295ft). One of the best spots to view the cliffs is from Bluffers Park, where there's a good beach, picnic areas, a restaurant and boat ramps.

➕ Off map to northeast

TODMORDEN MILLS

The old buildings of a mill established in the late 18th century now tell the story of Toronto's early industrial history. You can explore the former homes of the millers and see the old Don train station, the Brewery Gallery and the Papermill Theatre and Gallery.

➕ Off map to northeast ✉ 67 Pottery Road ☎ 416/396-2819 ⏰ Vary, call for details 🚇 Broadview, then northbound buses to Mortimer Avenue ♿ Few 💷 Inexpensive

TOMMY THOMPSON PARK

On a man-made spit of land that curves out into the lake, this area has been colonized by muskrats, woodchucks, foxes, coyotes, snakes, turtles and toads and around 45 bird species.

➕ Off map to south   Off south end of Leslie Street ☎ 416/661-6600 ⏰ Apr–Oct Sat–Sun 9–6; Nov–Mar Sat–Sun 9–4.30 🚌 97B ♿ Good 💷 Free

Bluffers Park Marina at the base of Scarborough Bluffs

Cannon outside Colborne Lodge

Excursions

KLEINBURG

Picturesque Kleinburg, on a wooded ridge above the Humber River, is a 19th-century heritage town full of lovely restored homes, specialty stores and galleries.

The Kleinburg Nashville Historical Collection, open on summer weekends, displays artifacts and photographs of the town. The big event of the year is the annual Binder Twine Festival, dating back to the days when farmers would come to town at harvest time to buy twine for their sheaves. It still has an old-time feel, with traditional crafts, and entertainment, and the highlight is the choosing of the Binder Twine Queen. The McMichael Canadian Art Collection is also in Kleinburg (▷ 97).

THE BASICS

www.kleinburgvillage.ca
🖶 Off map
🚇 GO train from Union station to Malton, then Bolton bus

MIDLAND

On the southern shore of beautiful Georgian Bay, this summer vacation hub clusters around the harbor. A short downtown tour reveals 34 huge historic murals on the walls of business premises. The most remarkable, 60m (200ft) across by 25m (80ft) high, covers a grain elevator on the harborfront.

Midland is also home to the only Canadian national shrine outside Quebec, the Martyrs' Shrine, commemorating eight Jesuit missionaries who lived among the local Huron tribe for 10 years until they were slaughtered by the Iroquois. The fortified mission, Sainte-Marie Among the Hurons, has been re-created on its original site opposite the shrine. Contained within a wooden palisade, it includes a church, homes, workshops and barracks, all brought to life by costumed staff. On the edge of Little Lake, the Huronia Museum has a reconstructed typical Huron village. From the European settlement there are military artifacts, furniture and art collections. Other attractions include the Wye Marsh Wildlife Centre and cruises around the thousands of islands in Georgian Bay.

THE BASICS

www.southerngeorgianbay.on.ca
🖶 Off map
🛈 208 King Street
☎ 705/526-7884
Martyrs' Shrine
www.martyrs-shrine.com
✉ 16163 Highway 12 East
☎ 705/526-3788 ⏰ May–Oct daily 8–9 💰 Inexpensive
Sainte-Marie Among the Hurons
www.saintemarieamong
thehurons.on.ca
✉ 16164 Highway 12 East
☎ 705/526-7838 ⏰ May–early Oct daily 10–5; Mon–Fri only in Apr and later Oct
💰 Moderate
Huronia Museum
www.huroniamuseum.com ✉ 549 Little Lake Park ☎ 705/526-2844
⏰ Mon–Fri 9–5, Wed till 9
💰 Inexpensive

NIAGARA FALLS

This natural wonder of the world is on most visitors' itineraries. The Canadian side of the falls gives a far superior view to the American and though the town is marred by kitschy commercial outlets, nothing can detract from the breathtaking sight of the falls.

The best way to appreciate the power of the falls is to stand at the very top, on Table Rock, at the point where a dark green mass of water silently slithers into the abyss. It is totally mesmerizing, if rather wet. When you can tear yourself away, descend about 45m (150ft) by elevator to the two outdoor observation decks directly behind the falls. Here, more than anywhere, you can appreciate the tremendous power of the falling water.

Don't miss the *Maid of the Mist* boat ride, which departs from the bottom of Clifton Hill. You board in calm waters (and don the waterproofs provided), then voyage right into the horseshoe and the turmoil of water at the foot of the falls, venturing just a little bit farther than seems sensible. Soaked by the incredible spray, you can look up at the huge wall of water plummeting down on three sides—Niagara means "thundering water."

A little way downstream, a bend in the river forms a huge whirlpool, and you can view it from above by riding the historic cable car or from below on one of the thrilling jet-boat rides. There is also the White Water Walk, a boardwalk right at the edge of the rapids. About 8km (5 miles) north along the Niagara Parkway is the Niagara Parks Botanical Gardens, which includes a butterfly conservatory. The 56km (35-mile) Niagara Parkway winds along the Niagara River from Chippawa to Niagara-on-the-Lake past orchards, wineries, parks and picnic areas—a joy for biking and hiking.

THE BASICS

www.niagarafallstourism.com
Distance: 130km (81 miles)
Journey Time: 1 hour 30 mins
🚌 Public Transit
Greyhound
☎ 416/594-1311
🏢 5400 Robinson Street
☎ 905/356-6061

The Niagara Parks Commission

www.niagaraparks.com
✉ Welcome Centers: Table Rock Centre; Murray Street; Clifton Hill at Falls Avenue; *Maid of the Mist* ticket booth
☎ 905/356-2241

Where to Stay

Toronto's accommodations range from
budget hostels and modest bed-and-
breakfasts to temples of luxury. Wherever
you stay, the renowned Canadian welcome
is going to make a lasting impression.

Introduction

Toronto has some of the finest and most innovative hotels in the world, and staying downtown can be more picturesque than in many other cities. Here, the modern high-rise hotels might have spectacular views over the lake, while modest, more economical bed-and-breakfasts will probably be in superbly restored heritage homes on leafy residential streets surprisingly close to the center, and conveniently located for all the major sights in the city.

Be prepared

The city has more than 35,000 hotel rooms to suit a wide range of tastes and budgets, and it is might be surprising to learn that it is possible to just show up in the city and find a room—even, perhaps, a last-minute deal on the price. That said, it's usually better to arrive with a reservation. The city can fill up when one of the major festivals is on, and advance online prices are often a lot lower than for walk-ins.

If you do show up without a reservation, try the Travellers' Aid Society of Toronto (www.travellersaid.ca). This helpful service can found at a booth in the Union Station (tel 416/366-7788), and is open daily 9.30–9.30.

Hidden costs

Be aware that quoted room rates may not always include local taxes: 13 percent HST. If you arrive by car, some downtown hotels with parking garages will charge a daily parking fee while others may charge for valet parking, which can prove quite costly so check in advance of your arrival.

HOME AWAY FROM HOME

If you are a family or group and staying for a week or more, it might be worth looking for a vacation rental—even couples can save money this way. Using the properties to full capacity, you could get a per person nightly rate of as little as $30 and make further savings by cooking for yourselves. Try visiting www.vrbo.com or www.airbnb.com.

Budget Hotels

PRICES

Expect to pay under $150 for a double room per night in a budget hotel.

312 SEATON

www.312seaton.com
Friendly bed-and-breakfast in Cabbagetown. Two rooms have bathrooms; all have internet.
➕ P4 ✉ 312 Seaton Street ☎ 416/968-0775 or 1-866/968-0775 🚋 506 Carlton streetcar

ALAN GARDENS B&B

www.alan-gardens-bandb-toronto.ca
On a tree-lined street with three cozy rooms offering luxury fabrics, TV and internet. Bathrooms are not all en suite.
➕ N5 ✉ 106A Pembroke Street ☎ 416/967-9614 or 1-800/215-1937 🚋 505 Dundas streetcar

BANTING HOUSE INN

www.bantinghouseinn.com
Church and Wellesley bed-and-breakfast with period pieces and Canadian artwork. Full breakfasts, WiFi and a garden.
➕ N3 ✉ 73 Homewood Avenue ☎ 416/924-1458 🚋 506 Carlton streetcar

CLARION HOTEL AND SUITES, SELBY

www.clarionhotelselby.com
A good-value hotel in a Victorian building. There's air-conditioning and WiFi, plus a fitness room.
➕ N2 ✉ 592 Sherbourne ☎ 416/921-3142 🚇 Sherbourne

DOWNTOWN HOME INN

www.downtownhomeinn.com
Clean, modern rooms with hardwood floors, air-conditioning and WiFi. Within walking distance to the University of Toronto and Yorkville.
➕ M3 ✉ 2 Monteith Street ☎ 647/342-1010 🚇 Wellesley

DORMS AND HOSTELS

In summer, university dorms provide fine budget accommodations. **Neill Wycik** (➕ N4 ✉ 96 Gerrard Street East ☎ 416/977-2320 or 1-800/268-4358; www.neill-wycik.com), **Victoria University** (➕ J6 ✉ 140 Charles Street West ☎ 416/585-4522; www.vicu.toronto.ca) and **University of Toronto New College** (➕ J3 ✉ 40 Willcocks Street ☎ 416/946-0529, fax: 416/ 946-3801; www.ncsummer.utoronto.ca) are all downtown, the latter on the main St. George campus. There are comfortable rooms and decent facilities (TV lounge, kitchen and laundry). **Planet Traveler** (✉ 357 College Street ☎ 647/352-8747; www.theplanettraveler.com) is a hostel near Kensington Market that's been restored with green eco-standards. It has basic but clean rooms, rooftop bar.

HOTEL VICTORIA

www.hotelvictoria-toronto.com
In the financial district, with 56 newly renovated, boutique rooms with hardwood floors, WiFi and coffee-makers.
➕ M7 ✉ 56 Yonge Street ☎ 416/363-1666 or 1-800/363-8228; fax 416/363-7327 🚇 King

HOWARD JOHNSON'S INN, YORKVILLE

www.hojo.com
Great location and good value with modern rooms. Includes breakfast, WiFi, a gym and on-site parking (for a fee).
➕ L1 ✉ 89 Avenue Road ☎ 416/964-1220; fax 416/964-8692 🚇 Bay or St. George

STRATHCONA

www.thestrathconahotel.com
Decent, if small, rooms at a fraction of the price of the Royal York right opposite. Coffee shop/ restaurant and sports bar. 200 rooms.
➕ NL7 ✉ 60 York Street ☎ 416/363-3321; fax 416/363-4679 🚇 Union

TOWN INN SUITES

www.towninn.com
Great value, spacious suites with kitchen and separate living room close to Yorkville. Facilities include swimming pool, sauna, WiFi and buffet breakfasts. Only the largest suites are beyond budget price.
➕ M2 ✉ 620 Church Street ☎ 416/964-3311 or 1-800/387-2755 🚇 Bloor/Yonge

Mid-Range Hotels

PRICES

Expect to pay between $150 and $299 per night for a double room in a mid-range hotel.

DELTA TORONTO EAST

www.deltahotels.com
Attractive modern hotel in Scarborough, with the bonus of a large pool with waterslides, saunas and fitness room, plus supervised kids' center.
➕ Off map to east ✉ 2035 Kennedy Road, Scarborough ☎ 416/299-1500 or 1-800/663-3386 🚇 Kennedy, then bus 43

DOUBLETREE

www.hilton.com
This large hotel has 486 renovated rooms, two restaurants, indoor pool and a gym, and is centrally located for visiting all the major city sights.
➕ L5 ✉ 108 Chestnut Street ☎ 416/977-5000 🚇 St. Patrick

EATON CHELSEA

www.eatonhotels.com
Large (1,590 rooms) but well run, with excellent facilities for children.
➕ M4 ✉ 33 Gerrard Street West ☎ 416/595-1975 or 1-800/243-5732 🚇 College

HILTON GARDEN INN

www.hilton.com
Conveniently located for all the major downtown attractions, this is an all-suite hotel with swimming pool, fitness room and free buffet breakfast.
➕ N5 ✉ 200 Dundas Street East ☎ 416/362-7700 🚇 Dundas 🚋 505 Dundas Street streetcar

HILTON TORONTO

www.hilton.com
Near the Convention Center with 601 rooms over 32 floors. Rooms are well-designed and comfortable; and there is an indoor/outdoor pool.
➕ L6 ✉ 145 Richmond Street West ☎ 416/869-3456 🚇 Osgoode

HOLIDAY INN BLOOR YORKVILLE

www.ihg.com
A modern hotel, with fairly standard Holiday Inn rooms, but in a good spot for visiting Yorkville and the Royal Ontario Museum.
➕ J2 ✉ 280 Bloor Street West ☎ 416/968-0010 or 0800/911-617 🚇 St. George

HOTEL OCHO

www.hotelocho.com
In between Chinatown and the Fashion District, this hotel has a pleasing austere decor of wood, brick, and local art. Bathrooms are all marble and granite.
➕ J6 ✉ 195 Spadina Avenue ☎ 416/593-0885 🚇 Mimico 🚋 510 Spadina streetcar

ISABELLA HOTEL & SUITES

www.isabellahotel.com
A historic and visual l andmark, consisting of an 1891 mansion and 1914 seven-story tower, renovated and turned into a boutique hotel.
➕ N2 ✉ 556 Sherbourne Street ☎ 416/922-2203 🚇 Bloor/Yonge or Wellesley

MADISON MANOR BOUTIQUE HOTEL

www.madisonmanorboutique-hotel.com
Nicely restored Victorian home with traditional furnishings in the 23 bedrooms, some of which have fireplaces. All rooms have en-suite bathrooms.
➕ J1 ✉ 20 Madison Avenue ☎ 416/922-5579 or 1-877/561-7048 🚇 Spadina

MAKING WAVES BOATEL

www.boatel.ca
A unique B&B, on an elegant converted trawler, with three state rooms, lounge, galley kitchen and covered deck. Comfortable rooms make for a pleasant stay. Open May to September only.
➕ D9 ✉ 539 Queens Quay West ☎ 647/403-2764

BED-AND-BREAKFAST

Several bed-and-breakfast organizations help visitors to find rooms in private homes from $99 to $150 a night.
The Downtown Toronto Association of B&B
www.bnbinfo.com
BBCanada
www.bbcanada.com

🚌 509, 511 to Exhibition
🚆 Exhibition

POSH DIGS

www.poshdigstoronto.com
On a leafy street just off the Little Italy strip, this is a fine Victorian house with four bright, contemporary guest suites, complete with full kitchens and separate bedrooms.
➕ G3 ✉ 414 Markham Street ☎ 416/323-1178
🚌 511 Bathurst streetcar

RADISSON PLAZA HOTEL ADMIRAL

www.radisson.com
Harborfront hotel with rooftop pool, bar and terrace. The 157 rooms are well furnished and equipped. Fitness center, two excellent restaurants and a bar.
➕ K9 ✉ 249 Queens Quay West. ☎ 416/203-3333 or 1-800/201-1718 🚆 Union

RENAISSANCE TORONTO DOWNTOWN

www.marriott.com
Out of 348 functional rooms, 70 overlook the Rogers Centre baseball turf. Pool, fitness center and squash courts.
➕ J8 ✉ 1 Blue Jays Way ☎ 416/341-7100 or 1-866/237-1512 🚆 Union

RESIDENCE INN

www.marriott.com
An all-suite hotel close to the Entertainment District and Rogers Centre. Each suite has a full kitchen

and lots of amenities. Some have great views.
➕ J7 ✉ 255 Wellington Street West ☎ 416/581-1800; fax 416/581-0255
🚆 St. Andrew

SHERATON

www.sheratontoronto.com
One of the city's largest hotels with 1,377 comfortable rooms. Efficient

THE COOLEST ROOMS

Hotel Le Germain (➕ J/K7 ✉ 30 Mercer Street ☎ 416/345-9500; www.germaintoronto.com) is a member of a small, very chic and modern Montréal chain. A bowl of green apples highlights the front desk and a fireplace warms the minimalist modern lobby-lounge.

The Drake Hotel (➕ D6 ✉ 1150 Queen Street West ☎ 416/531-5042; www.thedrakehotel.ca) is in a rundown, but gentrifying part of the city and attracts a hip clientele to its "crash pads," which are small but "ultra designed."

The SoHo Metropolitan Hotel (➕ J7 ✉ 318 Wellington Street West ☎ 416/599-8800; www.metropolitan.com). Expect sophisticated, techno-savy rooms with contemporary luxe style right down to the Dale Chihuly artwork and the top-class restaurant Diva at the Met.

service and four restaurants/bars make for a pleasant stay.
➕ L6 ✉ 123 Queen Street West ☎ 416/361-1000 or 1-866/716-8101 🚆 Osgoode

SUITES AT 1 KING WEST

www.onekingwest.com
Stunning contemporary suites and a health club in a landmark high-rise hotel. It incorporates the historic former banking hall of the Toronto Dominion Bank.
➕ M7 ✉ 1 King Street West ☎ 416/548-8100 🚆 King
🚌 504 King streetcar

WESTIN BRISTOL PLACE

www.westintorontoairport.com
One of the best hotels on the airport strip. The 287 rooms are well furnished and equipped. Pools and fitness facilities.
➕ Off map to north-west ✉ 950 Dixon Road ☎ 416/675-9444 🚆 Kipling

WESTIN PRINCE

www.westinprincetoronto.com
Set in 6ha (15 acres), 20 minutes from downtown in the Don Valley. The 400 rooms are serene. Katsura restaurant has excellent sushi and robata bars, tempura counter and teppanyaki-style cuisine. Also has a putting green, tennis courts and fitness center.
➕ Off map to northeast ✉ 900 York Mills Road, Don Mills ☎ 416/444-2511
🚆 York Mills

Luxury Hotels

PRICES

Expect to pay more than $300 per night for a double room at a luxury hotel.

FAIRMONT ROYAL YORK

www.fairmont.com
Rooms vary and the service can be a stretched during busy times, as there are 1,365 rooms. It features nine bars and restaurants—the Library Bar is noted for its martinis. Pool.
 L7 ⊠ 100 Front Street West ☎ 416/368-2511 or 1/800-257-7544 (reservations only) 🚇 Union

FOUR SEASONS

www.fourseasons.com
Located in the heart of Yorkville, this is the city's top hotel. The service is personal yet unobtrusive, the 259 rooms are spacious, elegant, comfortable and well equipped, and the facilities excellent.
It has a great bar, DBar (▷ 90), and the fashionable Café Boulud attracts a celebrity crowd
 L1 ⊠ 60 Yorkville Avenue ☎ 416/964-0411 🚇 Bay

HAZELTON HOTEL

www.thehazeltonhotel.com
Huge rooms and suites provide the ultimate in luxury, from granite bathrooms to in-room entertainment centers. There's also a fine dining restaurant, spa and movie screening room.
 L1 ⊠ 118 Yorkville Avenue ☎ 416/963-6300, 1-866/473-6301 🚇 Bay

MARRIOTT EATON CENTRE

www.marriott.com
Conveniently located, this hotel has 461 rooms with high-tech amenities such as a big-screen TV, a rooftop pool and two restaurants and lounges.
 L5 ⊠ 525 Bay Street ☎ 416/597-9200 or 1-800/905-0667 🚇 Dundas

OMNI KING EDWARD HOTEL

www.omnihotels.com
An architectural jewel in marble and sculpted stucco. The Victoria's Restaurant is a favorite gathering place. The 301 rooms are very spacious, well decorated and equipped.
 M7 ⊠ 37 King Street East ☎ 416/863-9700 🚇 King

PARK HYATT

www.parktoronto.hyatt.com
The 346 rooms have been renovated to an exceptional standard with fine fabrics and furnishings and the latest amenities. There are three restaurants—the chic, international bistro, Annona, a steakhouse, and the Roof Lounge, serving bar meals—and a still-water spa.
 K2 ⊠ 4 Avenue Road ☎ 416/925-1234 🚇 Bay or Museum

WESTIN HARBOUR CASTLE

www.westinharbourcastletoronto.com
Large 38-story hotel in a fabulous lakefront location handy for many sights, including the CN Tower, Air Canada Centre, and the Entertainment and Financial districts; many of the 977 rooms have a lake view. Well-appointed and comfortable rooms and excellent facilities—including Toula, for fine Italian dining, squash and tennis courts and an indoor pool—make for a pleasant stay.
 M9 ⊠ 1 Harbour Square ☎ 416/869-1600 🚇 Union

COUNTRY LUXURY

For a languorous and luxurious country-house experience convenient for the attractive Victorian town of Stratford, book a room at **Langdon Hall**. Built in 1902, it stands in 81ha (200 acres), with superb accommodations set around a cloister garden. The main house has a lovely dining room serving excellent food and a conservatory. Facilities include an outdoor pool, tennis court, croquet lawn, billiards room, spa-fitness center and cross-country ski trails.
⊠ 1 Langdon Drive, Cambridge, ON N3H 4R8 ☎ 519/740-2100; www.langdonhall.ca

Here is the key information to smooth your path both before you go and when you arrive. Get savvy with the local transportation, explore Toronto, or check out what festivals are taking place.

Planning Ahead

When to Go

The best time to visit Toronto is in summer, when Canada's Wonderland and all the other attractions are open, and the ferries to the islands are in full swing. Fall is also good. The weather is still warm, and outside the city the forests take on a rich golden glow.

TIME

Toronto is on Eastern Standard Time, 3 hours ahead of Los Angeles, and 5 hours behind GMT.

AVERAGE DAILY MAXIMUM TEMPERATURES

JAN	FEB	MAR	APR	MAY	JUN	JUL	AUG	SEP	OCT	NOV	DEC
23°F	26°F	35°F	47°F	57°F	68°F	70°F	70°F	64°F	53°F	42°F	30°F
−4°C	−3°C	1°C	8°C	14°C	19°C	21°C	21°C	18°C	12°C	6°C	−1°C

Spring (mid-March to late May) is unpredictable. Occasional snow or ice storms occur as late as mid-April.

Summer (early June to late August) is warm to hot, with occasional rain or humidity and cooler evenings.

Fall (September and October) has cooler temperatures, sunny days and occasional rain; the weather is ideal for exploring.

Winter (November to March) can be harsh. November is always unpredictable and mid-winter is much colder because of the unrelenting winds blowing off Lake Ontario.

SPORTING CALENDAR

Athletics
Toronto Waterfront Marathon: Oct;
Toronto Marathon: May

Baseball
Toronto Blue Jays, Rogers Centre: Apr–Oct

Basketball
Toronto Raptors, Air Canada Centre: Oct–Apr

Football
Toronto Argonauts, Rogers Centre: Jun–Oct
Championship games: Grey Cup (national), Vanier Cup (university) and Metro Bowl (high school): all late Nov

Hockey
Toronto Maple Leafs, Air Canada Centre: Oct–Apr
Toronto Marlies, Ricoh Coliseum, Exhibition Place: Oct–Apr

Horse racing
Queen's Plate Woodbine Racetrack: late Jun/early Jul

Lacrosse
Toronto Rock, Air Canada Centre: Jan–May

Motor Racing
Honda Indy Toronto, Exhibition Place: Jul

Soccer
Toronto Lynx and Lady Lynx, Centennial Park Stadium, Etobicoke: May–Jul
Toronto FC, BMO Field and Rogers Centre: Apr–Oct

Water sports
Dragon Boat Race Festival, Toronto Islands: mid-Jun
Great White North Dragon Boat Race, Western Beaches Watercourse, Marilyn Bell Park: early Sep

Toronto Online

www.seetorontonow.com
Toronto's official tourist website is run by
the Toronto Convention and Visitors Association.
Shopping, accommodations, attractions,
theater and restaurants.

www.toronto.com
A comprehensive Toronto guide. Good event
and concert listings, shopping information, plus
excellent links.

www.toronto.ca
The City of Toronto's comprehensive attractions
guide, with history and archive photos.

www.where.ca/toronto
Practical info and up-to-date event listings.

www.thestar.com and www.torontolife.com
Two good media sites with listings.

www.ontariotravel.net
The Ontario's official travel information site.

www.niagarafallstourism.com
Niagara Tourism's official site.

www.niagaraparks.com
Niagara region tourist information, focusing on
events and attractions.

www.goliveto.ca and tapa.ca
Toronto Alliance for the Performing Arts sites
listing all the theater, dance, ballet, opera, comedy and musical theater companies in Toronto;
links to box offices and ticket agencies.

www.ttc.ca
Toronto Transit Commission site, with details
about buses, subways and streetcars.

www.findtheway.ca
Information about transit systems for the city
and outlying areas.

GOOD TRAVEL SITES

www.fodors.com
A complete travel-planning
site. Reserve air tickets, cars
and rooms; research prices
and weather; pose questions
to fellow travelers; and find
links to other sites.

www.worldweb.com
A comprehensive travel
guide. Plan your trip aided
by online hotel reservation,
info about transportation,
weather, restaurants, events
and shopping. Maps and
photo gallery.

WIFI IN THE CITY

Toronto Reference Library
This is the best place to go
online. The banks of comput-
ers can be used for long or
short periods.
✉ 789 Yonge Street
☎ 416/395-5577 🕐 Mon–
Fri 9–8.30 💲 Free

Wireless Toronto
Provides free WiFi hotspots
throughout Toronto.

Free WiFi is also available
through the City of Toronto
at City Hall, at most major
TTC stations, and at the
Pearson International Airport.

NEED TO KNOW PLANNING AHEAD

Getting There

NEED TO KNOW GETTING THERE

ENTRY REQUIREMENTS

Citizens of EU and most British Commonwealth countries require a valid passport and return or onward ticket but no visa. Regulations imposed by the US Department of Homeland Security stipulate that US citizens returning from abroad (including Canada) by land, sea or air will need to show a valid passport or other documents as determined by the Department. People under 18 must have a parent or guardian letter stating a length of stay. If children are traveling with a divorced parent who shares custody, that parent must carry the legal custody documents. If children are traveling with adults who are not parents or guardians, those adults must carry the written permission of the parents or guardians.

AIRPORT

Pearson International Airport lies northwest of Toronto, about 22.5km (14 miles) from the city center. Billy Bishop Toronto City Airport is located on the Toronto Islands, just south of Downtown.

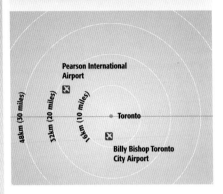

ARRIVING BY AIR

Pearson International Airport ☎ Terminal 1: 416/247-7678; Terminal 2: 416/247-7678; Terminal 3: 416/776-5100. Taxis and limos leave from arrivals level of all terminals. Fare is determined by zone; arrange in advance with dispatcher or driver. Downtown: $50; journey time 30–40 mins. Airport Rocket (Bus 192) departs daily 5.30am–2am to Kipling Station, Dundas Street and East Mall Crescent; journey time 20 mins. The 58A Malton route operates daily 5am–1am to Lawrence West Station; journey time 60 mins. Passengers arriving at night can take 300A Bloor-Danforth route (45 mins to Yonge and Bloor; or 307 to Yonge and Eglinton). Both night services run half-hourly. Ticket price is $3 (one-way). Contact Toronto Transit Commission (TTC ☎ 416/393-4636; www.ttc.ca). GO Transit has an hourly bus to York Mills and Yorkdale train stations (Terminal 1); Mon–Sat 6am–1am, Sun 9am–1am; journey time 30 mins to Yorkdale and 45 mins to York Mills (☎ 416/869-3200; www.gotransit.com).

Billy Bishop Toronto City Airport ☎ 416/203-6492; www.torontoport.com. Mainly used by regional airlines such as Porter Airlines (www.flyporter.com), which flies to various major cities in Eastern Canada and the USA. The ferry to and from the airport docks every 15 mins, daily 5:15am–midnight and takes 90 seconds. Free for pedestrians and $11 for vehicles (round trip). A pedestrian tunnel provides additional access to the airport. Union Pearson Express (UP Express) airport rail link service runs between Union Station (Downtown) and Pearson Airport (Terminal 1), with stops at Bloor and Weston GO Stations. Travel time is 25 minutes, with daily departures every 15 minutes.

ARRIVING BY BUS

Greyhound Canada (☎ 416/203-6942; 800/661-8747) to Toronto Coach Terminal (☎ 416/393-7911) at 610 Bay Street. Dundas and St. Patrick subway stations are nearby.

ARRIVING BY CAR

From Michigan, you enter Detroit-Windsor via I-75 and the Ambassador Bridge or Port Huron-Sarnia via I-94 and the Bluewater Bridge. From New York State, using I-90 you enter at Buffalo-Fort Erie; Niagara Falls, NY-Niagara Falls; or Niagara Falls, NY-Lewiston. Using I-81, you can cross at Hill Island; using Route 37, you cross either at Ogdensburg-Johnstown or Rooseveltown-Cornwall. Once across border, you approach Toronto from the west by Queen Elizabeth Way or Highway 401, from the east by Highway 2 or Highway 401. Boston is 896km (557 miles) from Toronto; Buffalo 169km (105 miles); Chicago 838km (521 miles); New York 801km (498 miles).

ARRIVING BY TRAIN

Amtrak (☎ 800/872-7245 in the US) and VIA Rail (☎ 888/842-7245; www.viarail.ca in Canada) long-distance trains arrive at Union Station, which is linked directly to the subway.

INSURANCE

Make sure your policy covers accidents, medical expenses, personal liability, trip cancellation and interruption, delayed departure and loss or theft of personal property. If you plan to rent a car, check your insurance covers you for collision, personal accident liability and theft or loss.

CUSTOMS REGULATIONS

● Visitors over 18 may bring in free of duty up to 50 cigars, 200 cigarettes and 200 grams of tobacco; 1.5 liters of spirits or wine may be imported by travelers over the minimum drinking age of the province to be visited (19 in Ontario).
● No firearms, plants or meats may be imported.
● Information from Canadian Border Services Agency ☎ 506/636-5064; www.cbsa-asfc.gc.ca

Getting Around

DRIVING IN TORONTO

The city speed limit is 31mph (50kph), and right turns at red lights are permitted unless posted otherwise, but pedestrians on cross-walks have priority. Seat belts are compulsory. Towing is among the parking penalties. Call Trip Info (☎ 416/599-9090) for details of road closures.

VISITORS WITH A DISABILITY

Currently 32 subway stations are accessible, with more planned. The TTC's bus fleet is entirely wheelchair and scooter friendly, as are all 170 bus routes. Soon all the streetcars will be as well. Visit the TTC website (www.ttc.ca). Wheel-Trans offers a door-to-door service (5am–11pm) for registered customers (☎ 416/ 393-4111, 416/393-4311 for hearing impaired). Parking privileges are extended to drivers who have disabled plates or a pass allowing parking in "No Parking" zones. Many buildings are barrier-free and well equipped with elevators. For more information, contact Toronto Community Foundation ✉ 33 Bloor Street East, Suite 1603, Toronto, ON M4W 3H1 ☎ 416/921-2035 ◷ Daily 8am–6pm.

Toronto has an excellent and reliable public transportation network, comprising subway, buses and streetcars.

SUBWAY, STREETCARS AND BUSES
● The subway is fast and easy to use.
● The subway consists of four major lines, Yonge-University-Spadina (1), Bloor-Danforth (2), Scarborough RT (3), and Sheppard (4). Line 1 has 32 stations and generally runs in a south and then north direction, from Yonge Street down to Union Station in downtown Toronto. Line 2 has 31 stations and runs from east to west along Bloor Street and Danforth Avenue. Line 3 is a rapid transit route and Line 4 runs east to west along Sheppard Avenue East.
● You need a token (sold in various quantities including 3 for $8.10, 5 for $13.50, 10 for $27, etc.) or a cash single fare for $3, which can be bought in any subway station. Drop it into the box at the ticket window or into the turnstile. Day, weekly and monthly passes are available. A day pass ($11) covers one adult from the start of service until 5.30am the next day, for unlimited travel on all regular TTC routes. On weekends and statutory holidays, the same ticket will cover a family: either two adults, or two adults and up to four children 19 or under, or one adult and up to 5 children aged 19 or under. The weekly pass costs $39.25 ($31.25 for students and senior citizens); the monthly Metropass costs $133.75 ($108 for students and senior citizens).
● Discounts are available for students aged 19 and under, senior citizens and children under 12.
● The subway system is connected to the bus and streetcar network. It is always wise to pick up a transfer at the subway station from the red push-button machine at the entrance or from the bus driver. By so doing, you can board a streetcar going east or west from the subway station if you need to, or transfer from the bus to the subway without paying extra. Transfers

are only available for continuation of a journey, and can't be used if you stop over in between.

● If you are not transferring, a bus ride costs a token, or you can pay with the exact change.

● Bus stops are at or near corners and are marked by elongated signs with red stripes and bus and streetcar diagrams. Pick up a Ride Guide map at subway stations.

● Be warned—bus stops are not always easy to see.

● The subway operates Mon–Fri 6am–1.30am and Sun 9am–1.30am. A Blue Night Network is in operation outside those hours on basic surface routes, running about every 30 minutes. Blue reflective bands indicate the bus stops served.

● For transit information pick up a Ride Guide, available at subway stations, tourist offices and other public places, or call ☎ 416/393-4636 (7am–10pm).

TAXIS

● Cabs can be hailed on the street.

● The light on the rooftop will be turned on if the taxi is available.

● All taxis must display rates and contain a meter.

● Tip 15–20 percent.

● If you need to call for a cab, these are some of the options:

Beck Taxi ☎ 416/751-5555

City Taxi ☎ 416/740-2222

Co-op Cabs ☎ 416/504-2667

Crown Taxi ☎ 416/240-0000

Diamond Taxi ☎ 416/366-6868

These, and a number of other companies, can also be reached via a connection service, ☎ 416/TAXICAB.

DRIVING

You need your driver's license, car registration and proof of car insurance to drive in Canada. Check the latest information on travel documentation before leaving home.

You can obtain information from: Tourism Toronto ✉ 207 Queens Quay West in Queen's Quay Terminal ☎ 416/203-2600 or 800/499-2514; www.seetorontonow.com 🕐 Mon–Fri 8–5. The visitor information center in the Atrium on Bay is open daily.

Anyone traveling alone on buses at night (9pm–5am) can request to get off between stops to be closer to their destination. If you require this service, let the driver know at least one stop before you want to get off. You will get off at the front, and rear bus doors are kept closed to prevent a fellow passenger from following.

Essential Facts

NEED TO KNOW **ESSENTIAL FACTS**

NATIONAL HOLIDAYS

New Year's Day (January 1)
**Good Friday and/or Easter
Monday**
Victoria Day (third Monday
in May)
Canada Day (July 1)
Civic Holiday (first Monday
in August)
Labour Day (first Monday in
September)
Thanksgiving (second
Monday in October)
Remembrance Day
(November 11)
Christmas Day
(December 25)
Boxing Day (December 26)

MONEY

The Canadian dollar is the
unit of currency (= 100
cents). Coins include 10¢
(dime) and 25¢ (quarter),
and $1 (loonie) and $2
(twoonie). Bills are $5, $10,
$20, $50 and $100. Stores
may refuse large bills.

ELECTRICITY

● 110v, 60Hz AC. US-style flat 2-pin plugs.

MEDICAL AND DENTAL TREATMENT

● 24-hour emergency service is provided by the
Toronto General Hospital ☎ 416/340-4800.
The main entrance is at 200 Elizabeth Street;
another entrance is at 150 Gerrard Street West.
● If you need a doctor, ask at your hotel or seek
a referral from the College of Physicians and
Surgeons ✉ 80 College Street ☎ 416/967-
2600 🕘 9–5
● In the event of a dental emergency ask for
a referral from the Ontario Dental Association
☎ 416/922-3900

MEDICINES

● Always bring a prescription for any medica-
tions in case of loss and also to show to the
customs officers if necessary.
● Shopper's Drug Mart (✉ 465 Yonge Street
☎ 416/408-4000) stays open 24 hours. Rexall
Pharma Plus (✉ 63 Wellesley Street at Church
☎ 416/924-7769) is open until midnight.

MONEY MATTERS

● Most banks have ATMs that are linked to
Cirrus, Plus or other networks and this is the
easiest way to secure cash. Check that your PIN
is valid in Canada. Also check on frequency and
amount limits of withdrawals. For ATM locations
visit www.mastercard.com for MasterCard and
for Visa/Plus, www.visa.com.
● Credit cards are widely accepted. American
Express, Diner's Club, Discover, MasterCard
and Visa are the most common.
● Traveler's checks are accepted in all but small
shops as long as the denominations are low
($20 or $50). If you carry traveler's checks in
Canadian dollars, you save on conversion fees.

OPENING HOURS

● Banks: Mon–Fri 9 or 9.30–4 or 5pm; some
are open longer and some open Sat–Sun with
reduced hours.

- Museums: hours vary.
- Shops: generally Mon–Wed 9.30 or 10–6, Sat, Sun 10–5. Hours are often extended on Thu or Fri until 8 or 9. Malls stay open later.

POST OFFICES

- Postal services can be found at convenience and drugstores. Look for a sign in the window advertising postal services.
- There are also post office windows open in major shopping complexes like Atrium on Bay ➕ L5–M5 ☎ 416/506-0911; Commerce Court ➕ L7–M7 ☎ 416/956-7452; Toronto Dominion Centre ➕ L7 ☎ 416/360-7105; First Canadian Place ➕ L7 ☎ 416/364-0540

SMOKING

- Smoking is banned in all public buildings, except in clearly designated smoking areas. All bars and restaurants are nonsmoking zones.

TAXES

- The provincial harmonized sales tax (HST) is 13 percent. This applies to most items including retail, accommodations, and food.
- There are some exceptions to the HST that are only subjected to a 5 percent tax such as books, some baby items, newspapers, etc.

TELEPHONES

- To dial outside the Toronto area codes of 416, 647, 437, or 905 add the prefix 1.
- To avoid hotel surcharges on local calls use a payphone. Some hotels offer free local calls.
- For long distance use AT&T, Bell or Sprint rather than calling direct. Access codes and instructions are found on your phone card. If they don't work, dial the operator and ask for the access code in Canada.
- To call the UK from Toronto dial 01144 and drop the first "0" from the number. To call the US from Toronto dial 1 plus the area code.

EMERGENCY NUMBERS

Fire, police, ambulance
☎ 911
Toronto Police Headquarters
✉ 40 College Street
☎ 416/808-2222
Rape Crisis
☎ 416/597-8808
Victim Services
☎ 416/808-7066
Lost property: For articles left on a bus, streetcar or subway, TTC Lost Articles Office ✉ Bay Street subway station ☎ 416/393-4100 🕐 Mon–Fri 8–5. If you lose a credit card or traveler's checks, report the loss immediately to the credit card company or the company issuing the checks, and to the local police.
All embassies are in the national capital Ottawa. The following consulates are found in Toronto:
UK ✉ 777 Bay Street at College ☎ 416/593-1290
Australia ☎ 175 Bloor Street East ☎ 416/323-4280
USA ☎ 360 University Avenue ☎ 416/595-1700

Festivals and Events

FILM FESTIVALS

Toronto and the movies have become inseparable, with "Hollywood North" attracting the biggest names to the city's studios and locations. A whole clutch of festivals showcases the new releases and recognizes the artistic contribution of those who made and starred in them. The Toronto International Film Festival (TIFF) in September is one of the most important film festivals in the world and the city is full of international celebrities. TIFF Kids International Film Festival in April shows intelligent movies for kids, and other festivals include the Hot Docs Canadian International Documentary Festival (April); the Toronto Jewish Film Festival, and the Toronto LGBT Film Festival (both in May); and the Italian Contemporary Film Festival (both in June).

JANUARY/FEBRUARY

WinterCity Festival Canadian and international musicians give open-air performances, plus indoor happenings including restaurant events. *Late Jan/early Feb.*

MARCH

St. Patrick's Day One of the largest paddy parades in the world starts at noon on Bloor Street (at St. George). *Nearest Sun to Mar 17.*

National Home Show The Direct Energy Centre at Exhibition Place hosts a showcase of homes and interiors. *Mar.*

MAY

Canadian Music Week For four days hundreds of bands play venues all over the city. Also a music industry conference, trade show and awards gala events. *Early May.*

Scotiabank CONTACT Photography Festival World's largest annual photography event with month-long city-wide exhibits from over 1,000 local, national and international artists. *May.*

JUNE

Luminato Festival A 10-day arts festival with music, dance, film, literature, theater and visual arts. Various venues. *Early Jun.*

North by Northeast Toronto rocks with 1,000 bands in over 45 venues, plus comedians, music movies, big-name speakers and related events. *Mid-Jun.*

Pride Toronto and Gay Pride Parade An arts and culture festival. *Mid-Jun.*

TD Toronto Jazz Festival Fun along Toronto's waterfront from Spadina to Sherbourne. Music, dog competitions, water sports, plus a wine and spirit festival at Sugar Beach. *Jun.*

Redpath Waterfront Festival Four (nonconsecutive) nights of spectacular fireworks choreographed to music. At Ontario Place. *Late Jun/early Jul.*

JULY

Canada Day Open-air concerts, fireworks and other events. *Jul 1.*

The Fringe Festival An eclectic mix of theatrical events. *Early Jul.*

Waterfront Blues Festival Three days of free concerts featuring the best blues performers, with two stages. *July.*

Toronto's Festival of Beer Around 200 brews from across the country. *Late Jul.*

Scotiabank Caribbean Carnival The city sways to the sounds of calypso, reggae, steel bands and soca. Exhibition Place and other venues. *Early Jul/mid-Aug.*

AUGUST

Canadian National Exhibition and Air Show Three-day air show. Exhibition Place. *Mid-Aug/early Sep.*

SEPTEMBER

Canada's Walk of Fame Festival overs three days of pure Canadian entertainment including music, film, dance, and comedy. Massey Hall and other venues. *Mid-Sep.*

The Word on the Street National literary festival featuring readings, storytelling and other events in various venues. *Late Sep.*

OCTOBER

Toronto Oktoberfest Get out your lederhosen and beer mugs. Enjoy traditional Bavarian fare, dancers, polka bands, and more. Ontario Place parking lot. *Early Oct.*

Toronto International Art Fair One of the finest and most comprehensive art events in Canada. *Late Oct.*

NOVEMBER

Santa Claus Parade A Toronto tradition since 1905, the parade is complete with colorful floats, marching bands, and thousands of costumed participants. Along Bloor Street West. *Mid-Nov.*

Cavalcade of Lights Be part of the lighting of Toronto's official Christmas tree at Nathan Phillips Square. Includes music, fireworks, and ice skating. *Late Nov.*

CULTURAL FEASTS

In this multicultural city, there are a number of excellent festivals relating to the various "old countries" and they provide a great way to learn about the cultures that are being kept alive—not to mention the wonderful food. They include the colorful Chinese New Year in Chinatown (Jan/Feb); Taste of Little Italy, based on College Street (Bathurstd to Shaw), in mid-June; Taste of the Danforth, celebrating Greektown and its food and culture in mid-August; the Festival of South Asia, on Gerrard Street East (Coxwell to Greenwood) in mid-August and the same neighborhood's Diwali celebration in mid-November; Bloor West Village Ukrainian Festival at the Harbourfront and the Hispanic Fiesta on Mel Lastman Square, Yonge Street, both from late August to early September; Roncesvalles Polish Festival, in the village in west Toronto, in mid-September.

DECEMBER

Tafelmusik's Sing-Along Messiah Fun Christmas event at Massey Hall. *Few days before Dec 24.*

CityTV New Year's Eve Nathan Phillips Square is packed with revelers. *Dec 31.*

Timeline

REBELLION

The first mayor of Toronto, William Lyon Mackenzie, shared immigrant aspirations for political reform and campaigned vehemently against the narrow-minded, exclusive power of the Family Compact—a group of ardent British loyalists who controlled the city's economy and politics. By 1837 he was advocating open rebellion, and on December 5 around 700 rebels assembled at Montgomery's Tavern. Led by Mackenzie, they marched on the city. The sheriff called out the militia, who scattered the rebels at Carlton Street. Mackenzie fled to the United States. Two other ringleaders were hanged.

Left to right: a polished stone Inuit carving in the Inuit Gallery; an ornate Inuit mask in the Bay of Spirits Gallery; an ancient Inuit painting, The Shaman's Wife, in the Kleinsburg Museum

1720 France sets up a trading post at the Humber River.

1750 Fort Rouillé (Fort Toronto) is built.

1763 The Treaty of Paris secures Canada for Britain.

1787 The British purchase land from the Mississauga tribe on which Toronto will be sited.

1793 John Graves Simcoe, Governor of Upper Canada, arrives and names settlement York.

1813 Americans invade, destroy Fort York, and burn Parliament Buildings.

1834 The city is named Toronto ("meeting place"). William Lyon Mackenzie becomes the first mayor.

1837 Former mayor, Mackenzie, leads rebellion against the Family Compact (▷ panel).

1844 George Brown founds The Globe.

1858 The Toronto Islands are created from a peninsula smashed by a violent storm.

1867 Canadian Confederation: Toronto becomes capital of Ontario province.

1884 The streets are lit by electricity.

1914–18 70,000 Torontonians enlist and 13,000 are killed in World War I.

1920 The Group of Seven hold their first art exhibition.

1923 The Chinese Exclusion Act restricts Chinese immigration.

1933 The Depression leads to 30 percent unemployment.

1950 Sunday sports are permitted.

1953 Metro plans under way.

1995 The Conservative Government is elected and focuses on budget cuts.

1996 *Fortune* magazine names Toronto "Best City for Work and Family outside the US."

1998 Toronto's six municipalities merge.

2002/3 Toronto Transit's new Sheppard Line connects North York to downtown.

2003 Distillery Historic District opens.

2007 A multibillion dollar redevelopment of Toronto Pearson International Airport is completed.

2010 Toronto hosts the G-20 summit.

2015 Toronto hosts PanAm Games.

BUILDING TORONTO

1844 First City Hall
1845 King's College
1851 St. Lawrence Hall
1852 The Toronto Stock Exchange
1869 Eaton's
1886 The Provincial Parliament buildings
1907 The Royal Alexander
1912 The Royal Ontario Museum
1931 Maple Leaf Gardens arena
1965 New City Hall
1971 Ontario Place
1972 Harbourfront development
1975 CN Tower
1989 SkyDome stadium
1993 CBC Building
2006 Four Seasons Centre for the Performing Arts
2007 Michael Lee-Chin Crystal at ROM
2008 Art Gallery of Ontario redevelopment
2015 Ontario Place gets a major facelift

An interpreter in 19th-century British military uniform in the grounds of Fort York (left); exhibit of Stone Age hunters in the Royal Ontario Museum (right)

Index

INDEX

Toronto 25 Best

WRITTEN BY Marilyn Wood
ADDITIONAL WRITING BY Penny Phenix
UPDATED BY Lisa Voormeij
SERIES EDITOR Clare Ashton
COVER DESIGN Chie Ushio, Yuko Inagaki
DESIGN WORK Tracey Freestone, Nick Johnston
IMAGE RETOUCHING AND REPRO Ian Little

Published in the United Kingdom by AA Publishing

ISBN 978-1-1018-7937-5

SEVENTH EDITION

SPECIAL SALES
This book is available for special discounts for bulk purchases for sales promotions or premiums. For more information, email specialmarkets@randomhouse.com.

Color separation by AA Digital Department
Printed and bound by Leo Paper Products, China

10 9 8 7 6 5 4 3 2 1

A05260
Maps in this title produced from mapping data supplied by Global Mapping, Brackley, UK © Global Mapping
Transport map © Communicarta Ltd, UK

The Automobile Association would like to thank the following photographers, companies and picture libraries for their assistance in the preparation of this book.

2-18 AA/N Sumner; **4c** AA/N Sumner; **5c** AA/N Sumner; **6cl** AA/J Davison; **6c** AA/N Sumner; **6cr** Imagestate; **6bl** AA/N Sumner; **6bc** Canoe, Oliver Bonacini Restaurants; **6br** AA DigitalVision; **7cl** AA Stockbyte Royalty Free; **7c** Tourism Toronto; **7cr** AA/J Davison; **7bl** AA/N Sumner; **7bc** AA/A Mockford & N Bonetti; **7br** AA/N Sumner; **10/11t** Tourism Toronto; **10c** AA/C Sawyer; **10/11c** AA/N Sumner; **10/11b** © Prisma Bildagentur AG / Alamy; **11c** © Arseny Barkovskiy / Alamy; **12b** AA Photodisc; **13ct** AA/N Sumner; **13c** © Robert Harding World Imagery / Alamy; **13b** AA/N Sumner; **14ct** AA/N Sumner; **14c** AA/P Enticknap; **14cb** AA/N Sumner; **14b** AA/N Sumner; **15b** AA Photodisc; **16ct** Canoe, Oliver Bonacini Restauarants; **16c** AA/J Davison; **16cb** Distillery District; **16b** Distillery District; **17ct** Tourism Toronto, Toronto Island Cyclists; **17c** AA/J Davison; **17cb** The Legislative Assembly of Ontario; **17b** AA/N Sumner; **18ct** Distillery District; **18c** AA DigitalVision; **18bl** AA/N Sumner; **18br** AA Photodisc; **19t** AA/N Sumner; **19ct** AA/J Davison; **19c** AA/N Sumner; **19cb** AA/J Davison; **19b** AA/N Sumner; **20/21** Torontonian / Alamy; **24** Reimar 4 / Alamy; **25t** AA/N Sumner; **25bl** David Giral / Alamy; **25br** Torontonian / Alamy; **26l** AA/N Sumner; **26tr** AA/N Sumner; **26/27** AA/J Davison; **27t** AA/N Sumner; **27cl** AA/N Sumner; **27cr** AA/N Sumner; **28l** AA/J Davison; **28/29t** AA/N Sumner; **28/29c** AA/J Davison; **29cl** AA/J Davison; **29cr** AA/J Davison; **30l** AA/N Sumner; **30c** AA/N Sumner; **30r** AA/N Sumner; **31l** Ripley's Aquarium of Canada; **31r** Ripley's Aquarium of Canada; **32l** Eden Breitz / Alamy; **32r** Eden Breitz / Alamy; **34** AA/N Sumner; **35-36** AA/N Sumner; **37-38** AA/N Sumner; **39-40** AA/C Sawyer; **41** AA/N Sumner; **44** AA/N Sumner; **44/45t** AA/N Sumner; **44/45c** AA/N Sumner; **45cl** AA/N Sumner; **45cr** AA/N Sumner; **46** Design Exchange; **47t** Design Exchange; **47cl** Design Exchange; **47cr** Design Exchange; **48** Distillery District; **49t** Distillery District; **49cl** Distillery District; **49** Distillery District; **50l** AA/J Davison; **50r** AA/J Davison; **51l** City of Toronto St Lawrence Hall; **51r** City of Toronto St Lawrence Market; **52t-53t** AA/N Sumner; **52bl** Textile Museum; **52br** Textile Museum; **53** Courtesy of Tourism Toronto; **53** AA/N Sumner; **54** City of Toronto St Lawrence Market; **55** AA/N Sumner; **56** AA/N Sumner; **57** AA/C Sawyer; **59** Centreville Amusement Park; **62l** AA/N Sumner; **62tr** AA/N Sumner; **62/63** AA/N Sumner; **63t** AA/N Sumner; **63cl** AA/N Sumner; **63cr** AA/N Sumner; **64l** Tourism Toronto, Toronto Island; **64r** AA/J Davison; **64-65** AA/J Davison; **65cr** Tourism Toronto, Toronto Island; **65c** AA/N Sumner; **66bl** Tourism Toronto; **66br** Tourism Toronto; **67** AA/N Sumner; **68** Tourism Toronto; **69** AA/N Sumner; **70** AA/N Sumner; **71** Brand X Pictures; **72** AA/C Sawyer; **73** Casa Loma Conservatory; **76-77b** AA/J Davison; **76-77t** Bata Shoe Museum; **76l** AA/N Sumner; **77t** Bata Shoe Museum; **77l** AA/J Davison; **77r** AA/J Davison; **78l** AA/J Davison; **78tr** Casa Loma; **79** Casa Loma; **80l** AA/J Davison; **80c** AA/J Davison; **80r** AA/J Davison; **81** AA/J Davison; **82l** AA/N Sumner; **82-83t** AA/N Sumner; **82tr** Royal Ontario Museum; **83cr** AA/N Sumner; **83t** Royal Ontario Museum; **83l** AA/J Davison; **84r** AA/J Davison; **84l** AA/J Davison; **85** Bill Brooks / Alamy; **86c** © Design Pics Inc. / Alamy; **87** AA/J Beazley; **86-88t** AA/N Sumner; **89** AA/N Sumner; **90** AA/N Sumner; **91** AA DigitalVision; **92** AA/C Sawyer; **93** AA/J Davison; **96l** AA/N Sumner; **96r** AA/N Sumner; **97l** McMichael Canadian Art Collection; **97** McMichael Canadian Art Collection; **98l** Torontonian / Alamy; **98tr** Canadian Wonderland; **98cr** Torontonian / Alamy; **99t** Canadian Wonderland; **99cl** Canadian Wonderland; **99cr** Canadian Wonderland; **100/101** AA/J Davison; **101** AA; **102l** AA/N Sumner; **102br** AA/N Sumner; **103t** AA/N Sumner; **103bl** African Lion Safari; **103br** AA/N Sumner; **104t** AA/N Sumner; **104bl** Courtesy of Tourism Toronto; **104br** AA/J Davison; **105-106** AA/N Sumner; **107** © National Geographic Image Collection / Alamy; **108t-112t** AA/C Sawyer; **108ct** AA Photodisc; **108c** AA Photodisc; **108cb** AA Photodisc; **108b** AA/S McBride; **113** AA/N Sumner; **114-125** AA/N Sumner; **124bl** AA/J Davison; **124bc** AA/J Davison; **124br** AA/J Francois Pin; **125bl** AA/J Davison; **125br** AA/J Davison

Every effort has been made to trace the copyright holders, and we apologize in advance for any accidental errors. We would be happy to apply the corrections in the following edition of this publication.

TITLES IN THE SERIES